pacific spas

pacific spas

LUXURY GETAWAYS ON THE WEST COAST

by Gina Hyams   PHOTOGRAPHS BY Cesar Rubio

CHRONICLE BOOKS
SAN FRANCISCO

LIBRARY OF CONGRESS CATALOGING-IN-PUBLICATION DATA AVAILABLE.

ISBN 0-8118-4617-2

MANUFACTURED IN HONG KONG.

DESIGN BY **AYAKO AKAZAWA**

DISTRIBUTED IN CANADA BY RAINCOAST BOOKS

9050 SHAUGHNESSY STREET

VANCOUVER, BRITISH COLUMBIA V6P 6E5

10 9 8 7 6 5 4 3 2 1

CHRONICLE BOOKS LLC

85 SECOND STREET

SAN FRANCISCO, CALIFORNIA 94105

WWW.CHRONICLEBOOKS.COM

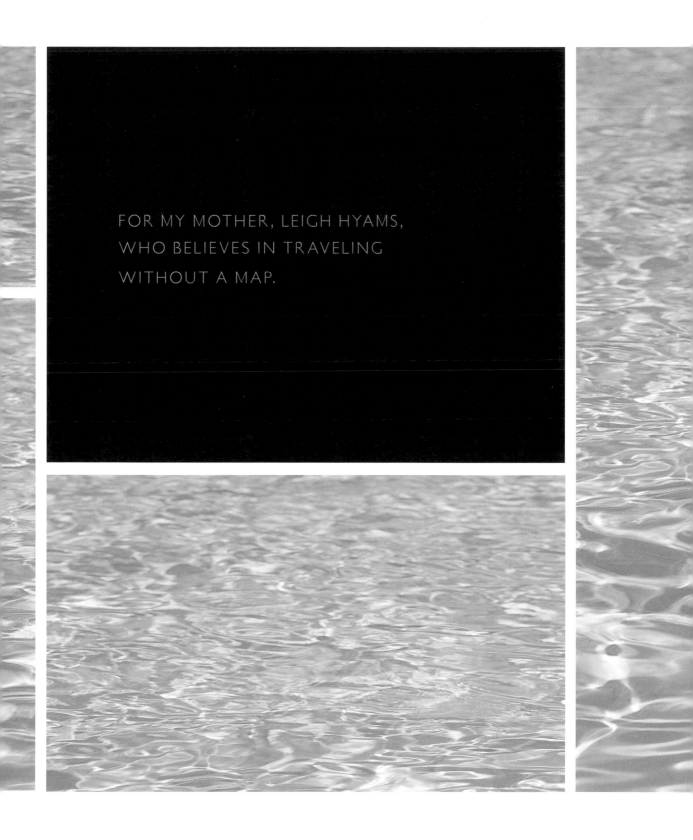

FOR MY MOTHER, LEIGH HYAMS,
WHO BELIEVES IN TRAVELING
WITHOUT A MAP.

TABLE OF CONTENTS

INTRODUCTION

Pacific Spas celebrates the crème de la crème of new spa developments on the West Coast.

Located in Baja del Sur, California, Washington, and Vancouver Island, the twenty luxury getaways profiled in this book are true sanctuaries designed to pamper mind, body, and spirit. You will find state-of-the-art facilities where massage tables move up and down on hydraulic lifts and lavender-scented whirlpool baths caress your body with a hundred modulated jets. These are places where battalions of pool butlers stand at the ready to supply plush towels and bottles of chilled mineral water and estheticians whisper to you in cashmere-soft tones.

At these resorts, you can restore your youthful glow with a caviar facial, have your chakras balanced with gemstones, do yoga on the beach at sunrise, sea kayak, hike in pristine wilderness, play tennis, or take a long siesta in a hammock. Cellular phones are turned off. You forget to check your e-mail. There are whales, eagles, and occasional movie stars to see. Housekeepers decorate the ends of toilet paper rolls with origami roses and place poetic quotations on your pillow at night.

The Pacific shoreline encompasses an astonishing range of geography, including mountainous desert terrain, tropical palm tree–lined beaches, vineyards, and old-growth rain forest. The spas reflect their unique coastal environments by incorporating indigenous ingredients, such as cacti, seaweed, grapes, and local mud, into their treatments. In addition, most of the destinations offer Asian-inspired massages and sophisticated European skin care treatments, yet the distinctive West Coast casual, friendly manner of the personnel leaves no doubt of your location.

UNLIKE SPAS IN THE PAST, THE TREND IS
TO DELIGHT THE SENSES WITH DECADENT
TREATS LIKE STRAWBERRIES DIPPED IN
CHOCOLATE.

Some of the destinations focus on holistic healing regimens, others on pure sensual indulgence, and still others on family fun. All manifest the highest standards of service. The staff members at these resorts are trained to both cater to and anticipate your needs. They will go to the ends of the earth to make your spa vacation fantasies come true, be it that you would like to learn how to cook delicious low-fat chocolate mousse, train for a triathlon, or return to your suite with your lover after dinner to find your bed festooned with crimson rose petals.

Unlike spas in the past that enforced strict dietary measures, the trend now is to delight the senses with decadent treats like strawberries dipped in chocolate. While it is possible to stick to a diet at most of these destinations, doing so is not required or even particularly encouraged. You will feast on the freshest of the fresh local produce and seafood, artisan cheeses, tender steaks, succulent poultry, fine regional wines, and, if you wish, more than a few lemon drop martinis.

WHAT TO EXPECT

Spa treatments generally follow a similar trajectory. An attendant greets you in the lobby and leads you to a locker room, where you don slippers and change into a luxurious bathrobe. You then unwind in the hot tub, dry sauna, and/or eucalyptus-infused steam bath before your session. Spas with co-ed bathing areas require swimsuits; otherwise clothing is optional in same-sex facilities. Your practitioner meets you in the lounge and guides you to a small candlelit room. Depending on the service you've chosen, you are asked questions about your health to customize your treatment. For instance, if you are pregnant, taking medication, or have recently undergone surgery, practitioners will take these conditions into consideration as they determine the best techniques and aromatherapy scents for you.

They then leave the room while you disrobe and lie down under a sheet. There is no need to worry about being exposed, as they make sure you remain artfully draped throughout the session.

If you are uncomfortable with the room temperature, depth of massage, music volume, or anything else, let your practitioner know during the treatment, so that adjustments can be made. This is your time, and your practitioner sincerely wants you to be happy. After the treatment, you are given a glass of water, instructed to continue drinking lots more water, and led back to the lounge, where you can relax by the fire and read magazines. It is common practice to tip 15 to 20 percent of the cost of your treatment. You can either give this money directly to your service provider or have it added to your bill to pay when you check out of the resort.

In general, these priceless spa experiences don't come cheap. You can easily spend $1,000 a day at many of these destinations. The fees for spa services typically stay the same year-round, but rooms can be had at a discount during low season. Check the resort Web sites for seasonal rates and packages. Alternatively, many of these spas are open to day guests, so you can enjoy treatments but forgo the high cost of onsite accommodations by staying at a less expensive hotel in the area. Be sure to book your treatments well in advance, though, as priority goes to guests staying at the property.

Pacific Spas is an invitation to journey to places where unspoiled natural beauty and nurturing therapies inspire states of being that feel like liquid dreaming. The profiles of these twenty singular destinations will draw you into the spa state of mind; contact information and specific treatment and activities recommendations are summarized in the Practicalities & Splendid Details chapter. As you peruse this book, close your eyes now and then, breathe deeply, imagine the waves lapping against the shore, and let the cares of the world slip away.

—G.H.

one&only palmilla

One&Only Palmilla rests on the tip of Mexico's Baja Peninsula, where the Pacific waters merge with the Sea of Cortez. Don Abelardo Rodriguez, son of a former president of Mexico, built the Hotel Palmilla in 1956 as a fifteen-room luxury resort. Accessible only by yacht or personal plane, the exclusive paradise attracted the era's most glittering stars—everybody from John Wayne and Bing Crosby to Ernest Hemingway and U.S. President Dwight D. Eisenhower vacationed here. Over the years, the property remained popular with wealthy clientele, but its storied glamour faded as the Los Cabos

region developed and competing properties stole the spotlight. That all changed, however, in 2004 when One&Only Resorts poured $90 million into a spectacular renovation, the centerpiece of which is a 22,000-square-foot tropical dream of an indoor-outdoor spa. Soon after its grand reopening, the hideaway was the site of John Travolta's fiftieth birthday party. This star-studded, margarita-drenched, much-publicized affair put the property squarely back on the jet set map.

One&Only–style pampering begins the moment you emerge from the airport gate and spot a sign with your name on it. Two waiting attendants, resplendent in hand-embroidered native costumes, place their right hands over their hearts and greet you with warm smiles. The Otomi people in the Mexican state of Jalisco use this gesture when welcoming a stranger to their home, and the resort has adopted it as the official greeting all staff members use whenever they see a guest. At first the salutation seems contrived, but eventually its relentless graciousness wins you over. The airport greeters whisk you into the waiting Palmilla house car (a gleaming Hummer), and en route to the hotel, play a CD of soothing guitar music and offer you refreshing iced towels, bottles of Voss Artesian Water from Norway, Evian spritzers, and ylang-ylang-scented oxygen mist. *Bienvenidos,* indeed.

The One&Only Palmilla spa sits adjacent to the historic Palmilla wedding chapel. The new building retains the traditional Mexican charm of the resort's original structures, with gracious Spanish Colonial–style archways, whitewashed stucco walls, and red-tiled roofs. It encompasses thirteen individual treatment villas surrounded by swaying palms, birds of paradise, orchid trees, and babbling stone fountains. Each villa features an air-conditioned massage pavilion that opens onto a private courtyard garden. Six double villas, designed for guests to share their spa experience with a friend or a loved one, have rain showers for two, outdoor whirlpool baths, and palapa-covered day beds strewn with bougainvillea petals. One deluxe spa villa sports a sensory float bed, a contraption that provides guests with the tranquil sensation of floating in water without the bother of

getting wet. If you like, spa services can also be performed in a cabana on the beach or in the privacy of your guestroom.

The One&Only spa menu of services represents a blend of Mexican, Asian, and European traditions. Many treatments begin with a floral footbath—a symbolic Balinese ritual that represents a cleansing of life's stresses and tensions in preparation for total relaxation. While you're seated in the garden, a massage practitioner pours jasmine-scented water over your feet and gently rubs your toes with a soothing mint scrub. Various "Spa Ritual" packages incorporate body scrubs or wraps, head-to-toe massages, and hydrotherapy treatments, including decadent Cleopatra-style warm milk baths and detoxifying seaweed soaks. Many of the rituals incorporate indigenous ingredients. For example, the Aztec Aromatic Ritual involves massaging the body with a pungent mixture of cloves, ginger, and cinnamon. The spicy scrub supposedly derives from an ancient Mexican village recipe; regardless of its origin, it smells delicious and creates an intensely warm, stimulating sensation.

The spa's massage practitioners are trained in a variety of techniques, including Aroma Stone, Balinese, deep tissue, prenatal, reflexology, Thai, sports, Swedish, and Watsu styles, as well as the popular Palmilla Four Hand Massage, in which two therapists

simultaneously stroke your body in perfect synchronicity. For the face, there are instant results-oriented skin care treatments, such as Japanese silk protein booster compresses, galvanic frequency, glycolic peels, and potent antioxidant vitamin serums. Daily fitness and aerobic classes are offered in the gym and yoga garden.

The KidsOnly children's camp offers full and half-day programs that include tennis and golf clinics, Mexican games, Spanish classes, sandcastle building, and a host of other activities. Also for young guests, One&Only Palmilla provides a "Your First Manicure & Pedicure" treatment, as well as special yoga classes for children and parents. Located on one of the only beaches in Los Cabos that is suitable for swimming, the resort also features two gorgeous infinity-edge pools. The new Aqua Pool, situated at the north side of the property, has a children's recreation area; the original Vista Pool with a swim-up bar has been designated for adults.

Acclaimed Chicago-based chef Charlie Trotter has opened his first restaurant outside of the United States at One&Only Palmilla. Called simply C, the sophisticated glass-enclosed dining room is bathed in water-inspired hues. Trotter's signature fusion cuisine changes daily to reflect the region's freshest ingredients; some examples of his wizardry include prosciutto-wrapped halibut with caramelized watermelon, daikon sprouts, and

mango-yuzu vinaigrette, and chocolate cake with *guajillo* chile sauce and butterscotch ice cream. He also oversees the resort's room service and Breeze, an outdoor terrace cafe that serves a light menu of sandwiches and salads. The resort's palapa-roofed third restaurant, Agua, celebrates the flavors of Mexico with grilled meats, fresh local seafood, and poultry garnished with regional sauces such as cilantro and lime or *mole negro*.

All guest accommodations at One&Only Palmilla have patios or balconies outfitted with sumptuous day beds and telescopes for whale watching and stargazing. The comfortable, elegant décor is rich with handcrafted Mexican touches like rustic wrought-iron candelabras and massive hand-carved mesquite beds. Guests also enjoy the latest amenities, from 32-inch flat-screen televisions and CD/DVD players with surround sound to high-speed Internet connections. The 106 new junior and one-bedroom suites are especially impressive, measuring 700 to 1,400 square feet, with heavenly bathrooms composed of smooth river stone floors, custom-painted tiles and sinks, and open bathing areas called "liquid temples" that have sculptural egg-shaped bathtubs, multiple showerheads, and big picture windows framing blue sky and sea.

Perhaps best of all, each guestroom is assigned a tag team of butlers who stand at the ready 24/7 outside your door to cater to your every whim—be it playing golf at the nearby Jack Nicklaus–designed Palmilla Golf Club, taking a romantic sunset cruise, or satisfying a midnight craving for chocolate chip cookies. They also manage the heady array of customized in-room amenities, noting things like your favorite fruits for the complimentary afternoon fruit plate, your pillow preference (there are five options), and even what fragrance you wish for the nightly aromatherapy turndown service. Depending on your mood, you might choose to scent your dreams with frankincense to promote balance or clary sage to spark joy and laughter. Night and day, One&Only Palmilla is a dreamy, luxurious pleasure.

Las ventanas al paraíso

SAN JOSÉ DEL CABO, BAJA CALIFORNIA SUR   MEXICO

Las Ventanas al Paraíso means "Windows of Paradise" in Spanish. The resort's brochure claims that "here, every wish, every desire is anticipated and fulfilled by caring attendants"—a boast that actually seems to be true. Since this Mexican hotel and spa debuted in 1997, it has drawn international acclaim for taking luxury and pampering to new heights. For example, the Las Ventanas pool butlers don't just supply an endless stream of margaritas and oversized fluffy towels, they also cool you with complimentary frozen chocolate sorbet cups and lemongrass popsicles; offer a poolside sunglasses cleaning

service (including, if needed, tightening the screws); provide iPod portable music players, magazines, and novels; see to requests for sunblock with specific SPF factors; and serve as personal alarm clocks, helping sunbathers get just the amount of sun they want. When the time is right, they awaken slumbering sun worshippers by softly playing an ancient Mexican percussion instrument called a *teponaztle.*

Visitors to the property are asked to fill out a guest profile prior to their stay, indicating a host of information, from preferences for food, drink, and music to any special reasons for their visit—be it rest and renewal, the celebration of a birthday, or setting the stage for a dramatic marriage proposal. Children are welcome at the resort, but most guests choose to leave their youngsters at home in order to best take advantage of the house specialty: all things *romantico.* Based on the particular vision of paradise the staff gleans from your profile questionnaire, they may suggest an outdoor Sea and Stars Night Massage for Two, an intimate, torch-lit dinner on the sand during which you are serenaded by a mariachi band, or an excursion on the resort's plush yacht, where you land on a pristine beach for a private picnic lunch.

The architects of the resort chose to embrace the stark natural beauty of the Baja Peninsula rather than to import a tropical or country club–like manicured landscape—the more common styles found at other upscale properties in the area. Echoing the region's startling natural juxtaposition of desert and sea, serpentine pools at Las Ventanas flow past sculptural sandy-white stucco buildings and through grounds sown with native

flowering plants, cacti, and succulents. This one-with-nature spirit permeates the spa at Las Ventanas in its serene Zen garden–like setting of raked sand and cacti and also in its Bounty From Baja signature spa treatments, which incorporate botanical blends of Mexican desert plants traditionally believed to encourage the body's innate ability to heal itself and to restore a sense of balance and calm. Chaparral, damiana, wild yam, plumeria, datura, elephant tree, turmeric, and desert lavender are among the ingredients used in the indigenous liniments, salves, massage oils, baths, and wraps.

The Nopal Anti-Cellulite & Detox Wrap is especially popular with the pool-lounging set. Locally grown, nopal (otherwise known as prickly pear cactus) is an excellent source of Vitamin C and amino acids. It is also believed to help the body pull fluids back from the tissues into the bloodstream, thereby diminishing cellulite and fluid retention. The 80-minute treatment begins with a dry-brush massage to exfoliate the skin and enhance circulation, then a freshly blended green nopal mask is slathered on and your body is cocooned in warm blankets to facilitate penetration and detoxification. A full-body massage follows, using a detoxifying cream and special skin rolling, percussion, and compression techniques. To further promote toxin elimination, at the end of the treatment the massage practitioner presents you with a (surprisingly delicious) frozen nopal-pineapple smoothie on a silver platter to sip at leisure in the garden.

Along with the signature Baja-inspired treatments, the spa at Las Ventanas offers an extensive range of both traditional and nontraditional therapies from around the world. The spa services menu is nearly one hundred items long, so whatever sensual indulgence or spiritual epiphany you crave, they probably offer it. You'll find French thalasso underwater massage, Indian Ayurvedic dosha balancing, and Javanese bridal fertility rituals, plus all of the standard massages, facials, and yoga classes that you would expect at a world-class spa. They even have pampering services for visiting pets. That's right: cats and dogs

AFTER ALL, LAS VENTANAS
AL PARAÍSO IS DESIGNED
FOR LOVERS.

vacationing in the lap of luxury can get their own stress-reducing neck massages and body-beautifying grooming treatments.

The meticulous handwork of local craftsmen is evident throughout the resort in such details as the impressive hand-carved cedar doors that open each suite, the colorful Talavera tiles, and the inlaid-pebble mosaic masterpieces that adorn the floors and headboards. All accommodations at Las Ventanas are incredibly spacious—even the smallest suites measure nearly 1,000 square feet, making them the largest standard guestrooms in Mexico. The rooms feature handcrafted Mexican furniture, Conchuela limestone floors, marble showers, terra-cotta wood-burning fireplaces, and private terraces with views of the ocean, coastline, or the verdant green of the Robert Trent Jones II Golf Course.

Healthful, gourmet Baja-Mediterranean cuisine can be found at the resort's three restaurants. At The Restaurant, the elegant palapa-roofed main dining room that sits adjacent to the infinity pool, you might select a vintage wine from the 2,400-bottle wine collection and then savor an *amuse bouche* of oysters au gratin with sevruga caviar, a flavorful heirloom tomato salad, and grilled bluefin tuna with onion marmalade and a merlot and *habanero* sauce, followed by a caramelized apple tart with vanilla ice cream for dessert. At the casual Sea Grill on the ocean's edge, you'll find Baja lobster tail, jumbo shrimp, octopus, and prime New York steak roasting on the barbeque. The Tequila and Ceviche Bar is another intriguing dining option. This outdoor bar showcases the bounty of the sea with a vast array of seafood (from sea snails to red snapper) used to prepare the raw ceviche, complemented by a selection of the most exclusive tequilas found in Mexico. Alternatively, you might just decide to order room service and dine in seclusion beneath a canopy of stars on your terrace. After all, Las Ventanas al Paraíso is designed for lovers.

cal-a-vie

Cal-a-Vie is nestled in 200 acres of wildflower-laced wilderness 40 miles north of San Diego. With a capacity for just twenty-four visitors and a staff-to-guest ratio of more than four to one, it is among the most intimate destination health spas in the country. Devotees return year after year to whip themselves into shape with the spa's super-structured diet and exercise regime. Cal-a-Vie feels more like a swanky summer camp than boot camp, however, as the rigors of the program are tempered with hot stone massages, collagen-papaya-green tea-paraffin facials, and deluxe citrus-scented manicures.

The current owners of Cal-a-Vie, Terri and John Havens of New Orleans, fell in love with the spa in 1998 after purchasing a week's stay there at a charity auction. The spa's reputation as a European-style Golden Door or a cozier Canyon Ranch was beginning to be compromised by its facilities, however, which were sorely in need of revamping, as they hadn't been updated since the spa opened in 1987. The rugged splendor of the Southern California landscape and the spa's Mediterranean architecture reminded the Havens of a Provençal village, and Terri made it her mission to refurnish and decorate the property with treasures she and John had found on their annual pilgrimages to Europe. Thus far, the Havens have invested $15 million to renovate the guestrooms and bath house, and build a new 17,000-square-foot state-of-the-art gym.

Guests stay in quaint cream-colored cottages with red tile roofs and forest-green shutters. The rooms are painted serene shades of taupe and sage and are individually decorated with French country-style antiques, imported chintzes, and vintage hand-colored botanical prints. Luxurious king-sized beds are piled high with fluffy down comforters and mountains of throw pillows. Private decks or balconies look out on chaparral-covered hills or gardens fragrant with jasmine, lavender, and roses. The rooms have telephones and CD players, but no televisions or high-speed Internet connections. The latter two amenities are available in the spa's Morning Room lounge, but they are purposefully absent from the cottages to help guests literally unplug from the stresses of their lives.

The spa supplies guests with a wardrobe of sweat suits, T-shirts, shorts, and robes, as well as rain gear, visors, and slippers. The clothing is laundered and replenished twice a day, so all you need to pack is a swimsuit, undergarments, shoes, and personal toiletries. Even the rich and famous wear the standard-issue comfy gray sweats to dinner, so there's no pressure to keep up appearances. By the second day, most female guests don't even bother to wear lipstick.

At the start of your visit to Cal-a-Vie, you undergo a thorough fitness evaluation based on body composition, a sub-max cardiovascular test, strength and flexibility assessments, and cholesterol screening. Both a fitness and a nutrition staff member analyze this information, along with the results from a wellness questionnaire. They then formulate a course of exercise classes, therapeutic treatments, and nutrition to help you meet your personal goals and desires. Though the details vary, everyone's schedule follows a similar cross-training arc, with strenuous physical activities in the morning, followed by rest, and then stretching, recovery, and winding down in the latter part of the day.

The day commences at 6:15 A.M. with either a hike through the hills or a brisk walk around the golf course, depending on your fitness level. Breakfast follows, during which a member of the fitness staff gives a brief "Fit Talk" to put you in the right frame of mind for the three or four hours of intense exercise slated before lunch. Every day brings a different mix of classes—you may have Pilates, spinning, and water aerobics one morning, followed by cardio-kickboxing, circuit training, and NIA (Neuromuscular Integrative Action, a

free-flowing, nonstructured, non-choreographed dance class) the next. "Revitalizer" breaks for the spa's signature vegetable and herb pick-me-up broth help keep you going. The tremendous range of exercise options and the gung-ho, supportive instructors make Cal-a-Vie a great place to try new workout modalities. Fortunately, if you discover that a certain type of exercise just isn't for you or that you simply need to rest, the instructors won't chase after you if you decide to skip a session.

Lunch is usually enjoyed alfresco on the patio by the pond-shaped fountain. Afternoon hours are reserved for pampering spa treatments at the Bath House and for gentle physical practices, such as yoga, tai chi, and labyrinth walking. Since the Middle Ages, labyrinths have functioned as prayer and meditation tools. Their maze patterns of concentric pathways that lead to a central spot and back again are a metaphor for the spiritual journey. Situated on a quiet plateau above the herb garden, the labyrinth at Cal-a-Vie is constructed of stones harvested from the property. It is intended as a peaceful space to quiet your mind and open your heart.

The sensual atmosphere of the mosaic-tiled Bath House was inspired by ancient Mediterranean, Turkish, and Roman baths. There you'll find Vichy and Swiss showers, a steam room, dry sauna, and a hot whirlpool bath, as well as massage rooms that open onto secluded decks for optional outdoor treatments. Two of the more unique spa services offered include the use of computer software to custom-blend aromatherapy massage oils for you based on your answers to a questionnaire about your personality, emotions, health,

SUPPORTIVE
INSTRUCTORS MAKE
CAL–A–VIE A GREAT
PLACE TO TRY NEW
WORKOUT MODALITIES.

and spiritual state, and Magnet Therapy Massage, where you recline on a magnetic pillow while magnetic pads are placed up and down your spine. The practitioner then uses a magnetic roller to stimulate muscles, boost blood circulation, and move energy throughout the body. This treatment is said to reduce tension while alleviating the pain and soreness of tired muscles.

With so much exercise, food becomes almost sacred at Cal-a-Vie. The chef monitors each guest's caloric intake, preferences, and allergies. The good news is that the meals are seriously delicious, including dishes such as baby spinach with orange-ginger dressing, Hoisin shrimp with low-fat lobster curry sauce over sweet potato purée, and a chocolate mousse ingeniously made with tofu. On Friday nights, the chef hosts popular hands-on cooking demonstrations to teach guests how to maximize flavor and minimize fat.

After dinner, guests gather in front of the fireplace in the Evening Room lounge for tea or "mocktails" and lectures on stress management, health, fitness, and nutrition. Because of its family-style communal dining setup and emphasis on group activities, Cal-a-Vie is a divine destination for people traveling solo or with groups of friends or family. Conversely, if romance or sheer indulgence is your priority, this may not be the spa for you. The ultimate objective of a visit to Cal-a-Vie is not to get a quick fix, but rather to leave the spa deeply rejuvenated, glowing with good health, and armed with the knowledge you need to continue on a path of healthful living.

montage resort & spa

The atmosphere at Montage Resort & Spa is pure sun-splashed Southern Californian casual elegance. Founded in 2003, the stately resort cascades down a coastal bluff in the picturesque arts community of Laguna Beach. The town's artistic roots date back to the early 1900s, when a group of talented artists settled here. Influenced by the French Impressionists, they explored the effects of natural light in their work, launching the California *plein air* painting movement. The essence of California was captured in these paintings, which highlighted dramatic views, lush landscapes, and rugged coastlines.

Montage pays homage to this bygone era with handsome Craftsman-style architecture and décor, and a museum-quality collection of early California fine art, sculpture, and ceramics that includes rare paintings by such famed *plein air* artists as William Wendt, Edgar Payne, and Jean Mannhein.

The horseshoe-shaped five-story hotel faces the Pacific, with the 20,000-square-foot spa occupying one side of the horseshoe, and a cluster of choice bungalow suites the other. Guestrooms are decorated in an elegant yet comfortable turn-of-the-century style with muted color schemes and classic details such as dark wood furnishings, period light fixtures, and authentic early California artwork. Sumptuous feathertop beds come outfitted with 400-thread-count linens and goose down pillows. Tasteful marble baths feature oversized soaking tubs with bath pillows, candles, and a generous supply of French bath salts; separate showers with shaving mirrors; and ultra-thick Irish woven towels, not to mention impressive water pressure. No matter which room you stay in, you'll enjoy an awe-inspiring ocean panorama, as well as views of the dazzling mosaic-bottomed pool, grand palms, and manicured lawns.

The resort is situated on a spot known to locals as Treasure Island, where legend has it that the French pirate captain Happolyte Bouchard buried chests of gold and jewels on its shore in 1818. Yet the place didn't get its name until the movie based on Robert Louis Stevenson's classic adventure novel, *Treasure Island*, was filmed here in 1934. The legend, along with the mile-long stretch of pristine white sand beach and the resort's three swimming pools (in addition to the central lounging pool, there's a glistening lap pool and a shallow children's pool), makes Montage a popular getaway for families from Los Angeles and Las Vegas.

Friendly khaki-clad pool attendants are constantly in motion dressing chaise lounges with towels, setting up cabanas, and fetching glasses of ice-cold lemonade. In the summertime, dedicated beach butlers stand ready to get games of volleyball rolling, dispense boogie boards and frisbees, book surfing lessons, and help unravel the mysteries of the tide pools. Another family-friendly aspect of the property is Paintbox, the exclusive children's club for V.I.K.s (Very Important Kids), geared to children ages 5 to 12. While parents unwind at Spa Montage, the Paintbox program entertains the kids with games, arts and crafts, balloon animals, treasure hunts, and more.

The chefs at all four of Montage's dining venues make extensive use of the area's abundant seasonal produce, catch-of-the-day seafood, fresh California cheeses, and farm-raised meats and game in ever-changing menus. In keeping with the surrounding community's artistic bent, food here is viewed as an art form, with the chefs serving as "artists in residence." Situated in a light and airy cottage on a 50-foot cliff overlooking the Pacific, the resort's signature restaurant, Studio, features clean, robust Mediterranean flavors and a wine list of some 900 selections that emphasizes California and French boutique wineries.

Spa Montage offers an array of comprehensive programs and à la carte services to refresh and invigorate your body and spirit, including skin care, hydrotherapy bath rituals, massage therapy, cooking classes, meditation, movement, and health programs. Rather than review a complex menu to decide which massage, wrap, or bath treatment is right for you, the spa encourages clients to "surrender" their cares. This innovative approach to bodywork allows the therapist to determine your optimum individual treatment. You simply

MONTAGE RESORT & SPA'S SPECTACULAR
OCEANFRONT SETTING IS A PEACEFUL SANCTUARY
THAT WILL HELP YOU RECONNECT WITH BOTH
NATURE'S BEAUTY AND YOUR INNER SELF.

book a block of Surrender Retreat time, which can be as little as two hours or as long as several days. The Surrender experience begins with a brief consultation to discuss your lifestyle, problem areas, and emotional state. The therapist listens closely and then prescribes the ideal treatment or series of treatments to heal and address your individual needs. Just letting go of control and leaving the decisions in another person's expert, caring hands is relaxing in itself.

The spa's practitioners specialize in holistic, noninvasive practices, and the region's lush natural habitat plays an integral role in the treatments. For instance, the spa staff mixes indigenous eucalyptus, lavender, orange blossoms, and citrus into many of its lotions and oils, and rather than rely on chemical peels, the Montage Anti-Aging Facial combines an antioxidant serum with a unique rigorous pinch-and-twist massage technique to stimulate collagen and increase the skin's elasticity. (The latter facial isn't exactly relaxing, but it certainly leaves your cheeks glowing.) Ocean-derived therapies include detoxifying seaweed mineral baths, anti-aging sea vegetable wraps, invigorating salt scrubs, and contouring algae cellulite massage.

The glass-walled fitness center overlooks the ocean and includes top-of-the-line resistance and weight-training equipment, cardio machines with built-in DVD players and televisions, and a movement studio where Pilates, aerobics, and other classes are taught. Yet the exercise activities that happen on the beach itself are the most fun. You can put your body to the test in Beach Bootcamp, a series of heart-pumping sprints, push-ups, and stair climbing, ending with a hardcore ab workout; begin your day with an invigorating Thalassic Beach Walk, led by a personal trainer who guides you on a barefoot workout in and out of the water; or conclude your day with the alfresco Sunset Yoga Ritual. Watching the waves break and breathing in the fresh, negative ion–rich sea breeze adds depth and serenity to any type of exercise. Regardless of the form your "surrender" takes there, Montage Resort & Spa's spectacular oceanfront setting is a peaceful sanctuary that will help you reconnect with both nature's beauty and your inner self.

Four Seasons Hotel
Los Angeles at Beverly Hills

LOS ANGELES, CALIFORNIA   UNITED STATES

Even if you don't arrive in a shiny black stretch limousine, when you step out of your car at the entrance to the Four Seasons Hotel Los Angeles at Beverly Hills, you feel like a star emerging onto the red carpet. The valet staff and front desk clerks treat all guests—famous or not—like V.I.P.s, and their extraordinary graciousness makes you feel like a million bucks before you've had a single spa treatment or glass of champagne.

The hotel is a favorite home away from home for the moneyed elite and quirky creative types, as well as for actual movie stars. Decorated in the manner of a stately

BE PREPARED TO DON YOUR
SUNGLASSES AND CULTIVATE
YOUR INNER MOVIE STAR.

European manor house, it's full of old-fashioned crystal chandeliers, extravagant floral arrangements, and elegant drapery, but the overall ambience is quintessential L.A. casual chic. Airy guestrooms and suites sport inviting peachy-pink and gold color schemes, bedding with stratospheric thread counts, and marble bathrooms stocked with thick terry bathrobes, green tea–scented Bvlgari toiletries, and stylish glass digital scales. French doors open onto balconies with views of Beverly Hills and greater Los Angeles.

Gardens, the hotel's celebrated fine dining room, features Florentine-inspired décor and dramatic red and gold furnishings. Four mural-sized eighteenth-century Italian oil paintings depicting the changing seasons provide the backdrop to views of the private gardens that border the dining room. The adventurous, eclectic cuisine, which might be described as Mediterranean with an Asian twist, includes such delicacies as butter-poached lobster with black-truffle flan, and crispy panko Thai crab cakes served with hot-and-sour dipping sauce and a delicious green papaya slaw. Windows Lounge, adjacent to the dining room, hosts a live pianist nightly and a jazz trio on Fridays and Saturdays.

As with all Four Seasons properties, children are welcome at the hotel, which offers complimentary bedtime milk and cookies and child-sized bathrobes. While there's no children's program per se, with four hours' notice, the concierge can arrange reliable babysitting services.

The Four Seasons Los Angeles Spa at Beverly Hills, which opened in 2000, is an opulent 4,000-square-foot state-of-the-art facility adjacent to the celebrated fourth-floor outdoor pool. An oasis of calm in the heart of the city, it is a true sanctuary for the senses. The first thing you notice upon entering the spa is how good it smells; seasonally changing aromatherapy candles set the mood.

The dreamy fragrances follow you from the reception area to the locker rooms and waiting lounge, where you'll find complimentary iced ginger tea, mixed nuts, and

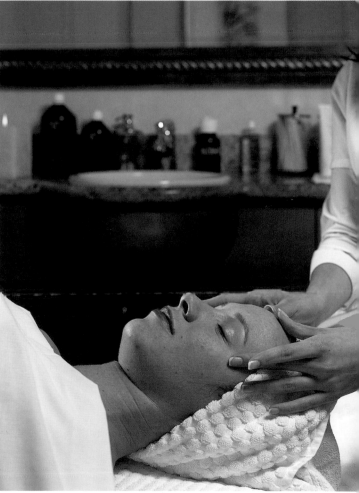

dried apricots and pears for snacking. The intimate spa has just eight treatment rooms—two for facials, one for manicures and pedicures, and five for massage and other full-body treatments, including wet treatments and wraps. High-tech touches include Bose surround sound systems in the treatment rooms as well as the sauna and steam rooms, and 10-inch flat-panel DVD monitors mounted under the face cradle of each massage table. The DVD monitors play "mood" videos of underwater scenes, rain forests, and national parks. Taking advantage of the beautiful Southern California weather, the spa also offers certain treatments outdoors in private poolside cabanas, such as the oh-so-indulgent California Sunset Massage (deep tissue or Swedish) conducted by candlelight.

Besides its stellar standard of comfort and service, what sets the Four Seasons Los Angeles Spa apart is its rich menu of California-flavored skin and body treatments, such as the Body Bronzing Massage, which results in an instant tan, and the antioxidant-filled Natural Spirulina Wrap, which takes advantage of all-natural spirulina algae harvested from pure salt lakes in Southern California. Especially popular is the Punta Mita Tequila Massage, where tequila and sage oil are blended together and massaged into the skin with long, deep, circular strokes. When applied topically, tequila is said to have healing properties, and sage oil is recognized as an analgesic that can relieve muscle aches and digestive problems. Many guests combine the tequila massage with a tangy Margarita Salt Scrub, a natural exfoliating treatment that blends pure essential oils of lime, orange, apple, and tangerine with tequila, sunflower oil, and salt. After these two treatments, you get to indulge in the healthy pleasure of drinking a virgin Margarita while relaxing in the spa lounge.

Skin care is another area where the spa services menu shines. In addition to traditional European-style facials, the spa offers a special Teen Clean Facial, using nutrients from a rare desert flower and vitamins from strawberry juice; exotic herb-based Mikiri (which means "deep" in the indigenous Australian Aborigine language) remedies; and a high-tech treatment called the Deep Skin Ionization Facial that involves a leather mask with metal electrodes. The "iderm process" employs a low-intensity galvanic current, which helps the water-soluble vitamin and mineral solutions penetrate into the dermis. This penetration reportedly feeds new cell structure, firms and refines skin texture, and minimizes bacterial growth. The metallic taste you experience as the current courses through your face is a bit disconcerting, but the results are truly fabulous.

After indulging at the Four Seasons Los Angeles Spa, overnight guests are invited to enjoy the rooftop swimming pool with its tropically landscaped garden, tented fitness center, and patio restaurant, the Poolside Grill, which offers both spa cuisine and hearty favorites such as cheeseburgers and lobster club sandwiches. Be prepared to don your sunglasses and cultivate your inner movie star.

the century plaza hotel & spa

LOS ANGELES, CALIFORNIA   UNITED STATES

Sleek, sophisticated, and sprawling, the Century Plaza Hotel is located in the heart of Century City on Los Angeles's fashionable West Side. The 19-story, 724-room concrete and steel high-rise was built in 1966 on what was formerly the back lot of 20th Century Fox Studios. The hotel is often referred to as the "Western White House," because every United States president since Lyndon Johnson has stayed there. The Secret Service, in fact, helped design the hotel's security system, which includes a secret underground walkway for incognito entrances and exits and bulletproof windows in the Presidential Suite.

The property underwent a comprehensive $70 million remodel in 2001 that renewed its sense of cosmopolitan panache, and included the construction of the huge and luxurious Spa Mystique. The 35,000-square-foot, Asian-themed facility is now the largest spa in Los Angeles.

Light streams in through dramatic two-story-tall glass walls to the hotel's marble-floored lobby. Check-in counters are off to one side; on the other is a cocktail lounge that faces a sparkling blue swimming pool and Breeze, the property's stylish restaurant. At Breeze, a favorite power lunch spot for entertainment industry executives, chefs concoct eclectic California cuisine such as fennel-crusted veal chops with white cheddar macaroni, tender organic baby lettuce salads, and crispy Point Judith calamari with saffron chili garlic sauce. The restaurant's décor is composed of elements that communicate a feeling of movement, from a flowing mosaic pattern in the terrazzo floor to bamboo leaves pressed in glass that suggest foliage blowing in the wind. The restaurant also features a striking green onyx seafood bar divided into two parts: one for succulent sushi and the other for fresh delicacies like clams and oysters on the half shell and bluefin tuna tartare.

The hotel's earth-toned guestrooms are comfortably appointed with contemporary cherry wood furnishings, high-tech electronic amenities, and chic Italian tile and glass bathrooms. Shower stalls are outfitted with snazzy adjustable massage dual showerheads that make for a particularly invigorating bathing experience. Each room also has its own little balcony overlooking the tropically landscaped grounds and offering sweeping views of the Los Angeles skyline.

Situated in the northern corner of the 7-acre Century Plaza Hotel property, Spa Mystique draws its inspiration from the traditions and rituals of Eastern cultures. Upon entering the building, you are enveloped in a serene environment of bubbling fountains, pale oak floors, and Asian antiques. Deep Japanese *furo* baths and a meditation garden beckon guests. Rattan baskets overflow with fresh towels, and iced citrus- and cucumber-infused water is in never-ending supply.

You can choose from an array of Asian treatments, including Shiatsu, Thai Massage, Green Tea Facial, and Lotus Flower Body Wrap. Spa Mystique's signature Korean treatment, Akasuri, involves vigorously scrubbing the body with a brush and ginseng body gel to prepare the skin for a warm oil application, cleansing, and a nourishing application of ground cucumber.

At the spa's Yamaguchi Salon, you can even get a *feng shui*-inspired beauty makeover. Founded by celebrated stylist Billy Yamaguchi, the salon offers manicures, pedicures, makeup consultations, and hairdressing services that employ the five elements of *feng shui*—earth, fire, water, wood, and metal—to create harmony between your physical presence and your personality. A Yamaguchi haircut begins with the stylist asking you questions about what colors you feel represent you and then explaining what those colors mean about your true self. For instance, according to Yamaguchi's theory, if you like purples and reds, then your dominant element is Fire and you're likely passionate and need a short, funky textured look, whereas if you're drawn to yellows, oranges, and browns, then your element is Earth, and you are probably a nurturing type who would be most happy with a short, simple cut or long hair with layers just around your face.

The spa also offers plenty of traditional spa favorites, such as Swedish, prenatal, and deep tissue massage, lavender- and tangerine-scented salt scrubs, a sugar body polish, and seaweed and mud wraps. Hollywood royalty favors the Instant Face-Lift Facial before special events. This treatment involves a battery of contouring potions that temporarily tone and tighten the muscles of the face, creating a rosy, youthful glow. The Twin Tigers Massage (two massage practitioners at once) is another quintessential L.A. experience— especially when you receive it in one of the outdoor cabanas surrounded by potted palms and banana trees.

Because the Century Plaza Hotel hosts many conventions, the spa caters well to the needs of frazzled business travelers. The 25-minute Hayaku Neck, Back, and Shoulder Massage provides quick relief to those guests with a limited amount of time. As men make up approximately one third of the spa's clientele (an unusually high percentage), there are a number of treatments designed for them, including sport-specific massages, polish-free pedicures, and the Mystique Yang Facial, intended to help prevent razor burn, skin sensitivity, and folliculitis.

The spa also features a state-of-the-art fitness area, complete with a full range of weights and cardio equipment, plus a yoga studio that hosts some five different styles of yoga classes. You can try introductory Yoga Basics, relaxing Restorative Yoga, abdominal-strengthening Core Yoga, mind-body balancing Hatha Yoga, or Vinyasa Yoga, which the spa describes as "a dynamic combination of strength, sweat, and spirituality."

Between sybaritic indulgences, strength training, and yoga classes, you can wander in your robe into the spa's Café Mystique for a nonfat brownie or homemade energy bar snack, or sip an herbal tonic in the Tranquility Lounge. The "Virtual Buddha" peach-flavored tonic is especially delicious; its mysterious herbs are said to awaken creativity. At Spa Mystique, beauty, health, and spiritual enlightenment fuse in glorious Southern California fashion. You will emerge from this spa experience feeling splendid, both inside and out.

AT SPA MYSTIQUE, BEAUTY, HEALTH, AND SPIRITUAL ENLIGHTENMENT FUSE IN GLORIOUS SOUTHERN CALIFORNIA FASHION.

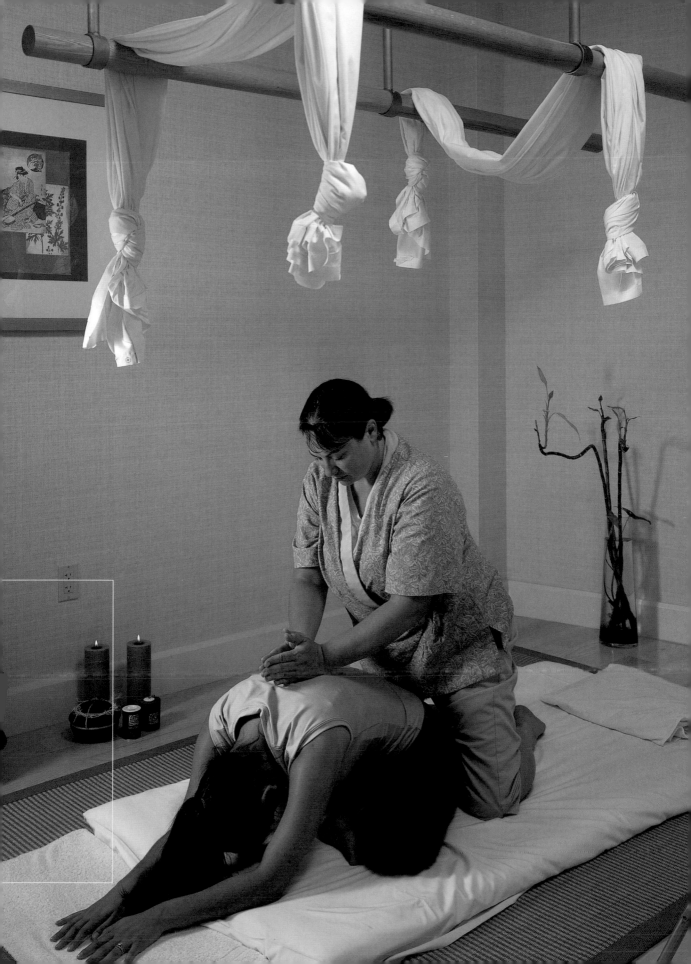

ventana inn & spa

BIG SUR, CALIFORNIA   UNITED STATES

The haunting and mysterious landscape of Big Sur on the central coast of California has inspired generations of artists, lovers, and spiritual seekers. Here the rugged Santa Lucia Mountains meet the Pacific Ocean, creating one of the most staggering coastlines in the world. The startling juxtaposition of natural elements has been described by many a hippie as "a sort of yin-yang unity of cosmic beauty."

Ventana Inn was conceived by movie producer Lawrence A. Spector as a back-to-nature retreat in the 1970s and was built with profits he made on the counterculture

classic *Easy Rider*. Stars like Steve McQueen and Ali McGraw frequented the inn in its infancy. Over the years, the property has become famous for its rustic sophistication and romantic allure. It remains a favored hideaway for Hollywood denizens, who go there to relax rather than to be seen.

The resort is structured as a haven for couples. To maintain an atmosphere of tranquility and romance, the management strongly encourages guests to leave their children at home. The sixty-two guestrooms and suites feel like luxurious tree houses, perched 1,200 feet above the ocean on 243 acres of Big Sur wilderness. The rough-hewn, weathered cedar buildings blend unobtrusively with the grassy meadows and riotously overgrown hillside forests of coastal redwoods, oaks, and bay laurel trees. Before your arrival, the concierge will happily stock your room with fresh-cut long-stem roses, lavender-infused massage oil, chilled bottles of Veuve Clicquot Champagne, or anything else you might desire.

In 2004, the management renovated the guestrooms, adding modern amenities like high-speed Internet connections and plasma screen televisions, while staying true to the original unpretentious spirit of the place. You'll find an earthy palette of sage, cream, rust, deep browns, and soft gold tones. These colors, which mirror those seen naturally in the area, are complemented by dark wood, granite, slate, and wrought-iron accents. Custom-made massive four-poster beds have hidden storage compartments that house folding tables for in-room massages. All of the rooms have wood-burning fireplaces and private decks that are discreetly screened with lattice and hedges, so if you want to sunbathe *au natural*, you certainly can. The larger suites even have outdoor hot tubs.

There are two heated swimming pools, each 4 feet deep and 75 feet in length, with adjoining bathhouses containing Japanese hot baths. The clothing-optional baths are especially atmospheric at night, when they can be enjoyed by moonlight under a canopy of stars.

The Allegria Spa at Ventana was established in 1999. *Allegria* means "happiness" in Spanish, and here it's a happiness derived from a balance of body, mind, and spirit. The most unusual spa services offered are Astrology Readings, in which you explore the meaning of your birth chart, and Color Readings, where you learn about the colors of your aura. The latter treatment feels like a cross between a psychotherapy session and a psychic reading. First you intuitively select four (out of 103) "equilibrium bottles," each containing two rainbow-colored liquids. The upper layer of color contains essential oils, while the lower holds herbal extracts, crystals, gem elixirs, and water. The healer explains how the colors you choose and the sequence in which you select them speak to your innate potential, the challenges you face, your present purpose in life, and your future potential. At the end of the session, she gives you a keepsake watercolor portrait of your reading.

ON A CLEAR DAY THE
PANORAMIC VIEW OF
THE OCEAN STRETCHES
FOR 50 MILES.

The more traditional spa treatments offer themes from nature: "From the Ocean" (salt and seaweed), "From the Earth" (clays and mud), "From the Plants and Flowers" (aromatherapy), and "Heart Centered Healing" (energy work, such as polarity and reiki). For the perennially popular Ventana Signature Aromatherapy Massage, the massage practitioner customizes an eclectic blend of modalities, including Swedish, deep tissue, Esalen-style stretching, and energy work, to address your specific needs.

Complimentary guided hikes and classes in a variety of practices, such as yoga, tai chi, and meditation, are offered daily. Many of these classes are also available as personal instruction in the privacy of your guest suite. The resort also regularly hosts weekend workshops in subjects such as *plein air* painting, photography, cooking, and mushroom hunting.

Whale watching, another favorite activity here, is best done in November, December, and January, when the southward migration of the California gray whale takes place. These marvelous creatures travel some 7,000 miles from the Arctic waters to the lagoons of Baja California, where they give birth to their calves. The playful whales can be seen from shore, spouting and leaping from the water. Sometimes they come so close, you can see them wink.

Cielo, the inn's restaurant, is reached via an enchanting 15-minute stroll along a winding trail that takes you through groves of towering redwoods, across a few wooden bridges, and past hillsides fragrant with lavender, sage, and wild honeysuckle. Shuttle

service is also available in inclement weather or by request. *Cielo* means "heaven" or "sky," and since the restaurant is situated at the edge of a cliff, it indeed feels like heaven there. On a clear day the panoramic view of the ocean stretches for 50 miles.

A bold spirit of innovation informs the California cuisine at Cielo, beginning with the cocktail menu, which includes twenty-two different kinds of martinis—from key-lime pie martinis with a graham cracker crumb rim to "Truffled Feathers" made with black truffle–infused vodka to martinis made with rose petal and cucumber–infused gin. Lunch and dinner menus draw inspiration from the flavors of France, Italy, North Africa, and the Middle East. Examples include seared Monterey prawns in charmoula vinaigrette or slow-cooked rabbit with red Zinfandel and dried plums served with sun-dried tomato rosemary polenta, baby carrots, and turnips. An award-winning wine list features California and imported selections, with a focus on central coast wineries. For dessert, you might try the trio of exotic homemade ice creams: roasted oak, lemon verbena, and red beet.

In a 1978 profile in *Architectural Digest*, Ventana Inn founder Lawrence A. Spector said he had heeded guests' request to not install tennis courts. "We don't encourage people to get into any kind of competition," he said. "We ask them to go out and walk, look, contemplate. We'll pack a picnic basket and send them out on their own. . . . In Spanish, *ventana* means 'window.' We provide a window to Big Sur, and that is spectacular enough. The other window is an introspective one."

Bernardus Lodge

CARMEL VALLEY, CALIFORNIA   UNITED STATES

"A jug of wine, a loaf of bread and thou . . ." is a popular line of verse taken quite literally at Bernardus Lodge. Bernardus "Ben" Pon, the resort's Dutch owner and namesake, winemaker, and bon vivant, wanted to create a retreat where discerning people could go to reward themselves with simple pleasures of the highest quality: exceptional, innovative cuisine paired with the finest wine; revitalizing spa treatments using natural elixirs; and top-of-the-line amenities that evoke an understated Old World elegance— all enhanced by Carmel Valley's pastoral setting and mild, sunny weather. With these

guiding principles in mind, he transformed a rundown hunting lodge that had been a hideaway for Hollywood types in the 1930s into a quaint French Country–style village.

Set on a terraced hillside, just inland of Carmel-by-the-Sea on the Monterey Peninsula, Bernardus Lodge is bordered by vineyards and the Santa Lucia Mountains. This picturesque region is known for its championship golf courses (there are ten such courses nearby) and, in recent years, for its up-and-coming wineries that specialize in Bordeaux-style Merlots, Cabernet Sauvignons, and Sauvignon Blancs.

The resort's fifty-seven guestrooms have vaulted beamed ceilings, overstuffed sofas and chairs, antique armoires, and gas-burning fireplaces crafted from Carmel Valley limestone. King-sized featherbeds are topped with Italian linens and fluffy down comforters. Hand-tinted botanical prints and large-format photographs of local vineyards adorn the walls. French doors open onto patios or balconies offering sweeping views of the rose garden, mountains, or manicured croquet lawn and bocce ball court. Best of all are the gratis "wine grotto" mini bars in each of the rooms, stocked with gourmet cookies, chips and salsa, crackers and imported cheeses, and three—count 'em, *three*—bottles of Bernardus Winery wine to celebrate your arrival.

The mini bars are just the start of Bernardus Lodge's culinary wonders. You have your choice of two restaurants: Marinus and Wickets Bistro. Marinus features California-French cuisine using local seasonal produce as well as regional seafood and artisan-

farmed meats. The chef's cooking style aims to enhance the pure flavors of his pristine, hand-selected ingredients. He eschews heavy sauces, seeking instead to let the naturally occurring flavors stand alone. You can feast on savory dishes such as white truffle risotto and pancetta-wrapped venison with chanterelle mushrooms, accompanied by a sweet potato puree and huckleberry sauce.

Wickets offers casual bistro-style fare, including wood-fired pizzas and an assortment of salads and seafood. You can dine indoors, where memorabilia from owner Ben Pon's race car–driving and Olympic feats (he was a skeet shooting champion) is on display, or outdoors under an expansive trellis overlooking the resort's croquet lawn.

The resort's chef hosts an intriguing series of cooking classes and food and wine specialty dinners throughout the year. Recent events include courses on seasonal cake decorating, honey infusions, the scent of food, decadent chocolate recipes, and a lunch made with thirty kinds of heirloom tomatoes.

The restaurants aren't the only places where local foodstuffs come into play. Indigenous herbs, flowers, essential oils, and healing waters are incorporated into the spa's treatments, too. The spa features a repertoire of therapies that utilize herbs unique to each season. For instance, during summer, skin tends to get more exposure to heat and sun, so the spa staff recommends a Chamomile and Rose Facial to help soothe sensitive or sunburned conditions and provide a natural hydration boost to your skin in the drier, warm-weather months. In the fall, they suggest a Lavender Fields Body Exfoliation in which

crushed, fragrant lavender buds are used to exfoliate and refresh the skin. After the flowers are rinsed off, a massage with the spa's own blend of lavender, bay, and eucalyptus oil helps to drain your lymph system, decongest your sinuses, and warm your muscles.

So many golfers visit Bernardus Lodge that the spa has devised several treatments specifically for them. The Aprés Golf Massage incorporates a special blend of rosemary, birch, and other therapeutic oils, perfect after a hard day on the links. La Stone River Rock Massage uses warmed river stones to provide heat therapy for aching and tight muscles. Sole Revival begins with a rejuvenating foot soak in a copper basin filled with hot water, fresh mint, rosemary, and rose petals, followed by an invigorating scrub, then a reflexology massage with essential oils, ending with your feet enveloped in moist-heat booties to allow for the deep penetration of skin-conditioning oils and ultimate relaxation. These dreamy treatments are good for tuckered-out hikers and bocce ball players as well.

The spa's most popular treatment is tailored for lovers. The Vineyard Romance Experience takes place in a room with two treatment tables, a two-person shower, and French doors leading to an outdoor therapy bath and private meditation garden. First, two massage practitioners scrub you and your lover's bodies with a mixture of finely ground grape seeds and red wine. Grape seeds are known for their high antioxidant content, which helps to heal the skin and prevent aging. You both rinse off in the shower and then steep together in an alfresco lavender aromatherapy bath. The treatment finishes with a warm grape seed oil massage. Afterward, it's impossible for the two of you to feel anything but blissful gratitude for life's finer pleasures.

SO MANY GOLFERS VISIT BERNARDUS
LODGE THAT THE SPA HAS DEVISED SEVERAL
TREATMENTS SPECIFICALLY FOR THEM.

The Huntington Hotel & Nob Hill Spa

SAN FRANCISCO, CALIFORNIA   UNITED STATES

Founded in 1924, the Huntington Hotel sits on the crest of San Francisco's fabled Nob Hill. The Georgian-style red brick, ivy-covered hotel exudes Old World opulence with antique European furnishings, crystal chandeliers, and elaborate drapery. Renowned for its discreet and gracious personal service, the Huntington has sheltered dignitaries ranging from Princess Grace and Cary Grant to Pablo Picasso, Luciano Pavarotti, and rock star Bono. The concierge welcomes all guests, regardless of their stature, on the night of their arrival with a complimentary glass of sherry or formal tea service presented on a silver platter.

The Huntington was originally constructed as a posh apartment house, so the guestrooms and suites are especially spacious and comfortable; several even have kitchenettes. Each room is individually appointed with classically elegant furnishings and original works of art. Many face panoramic views of the San Francisco skyline and bay. You can open your window and hear the clanking of San Francisco's famous cable cars and the chiming of Grace Cathedral's bells.

Big Four Restaurant is located adjacent to the hotel lobby. This establishment is named after the nation's four most notorious railroad tycoons of the nineteenth century—C.P. Huntington, Charles Crocker, Leland Stanford, and Mark Hopkins—all of whom built mansions on Nob Hill. Appointed with lead-glass mirrors, dark wood paneling, forest-green banquettes, and an impressive collection of original artifacts, historical photographs, and memorabilia from California's history, the restaurant's clubby atmosphere instantly transports you to an earlier era. The chef specializes in hearty comfort food, such as chicken pot pie, Irish lamb stew, and sautéed filet mignon with baby porcini mushrooms, roasted vegetables, and porcini-cognac cream. Nightly wild-game specials include caribou, wild boar chops, buffalo, ostrich, antelope, alligator, and occasionally rattlesnake. Desserts are equally robust: crème brûleé with fresh berries, warm apple walnut crisp, and bread and butter pudding laced with Grand Marnier custard sauce.

In contrast to the traditional character of the hotel, the Nob Hill Spa (which opened in 2001) is a light and airy, thoroughly modern, *feng shui*–enhanced blend of glass, steel, chrome, and marble. Floor-to-ceiling windows, sleek teak furnishings, and potted palms surround a stunning indoor infinity-edged pool. The white terrazzo floor is graced with a swirling mosaic of celadon tiles and ribbons of 24-karat gold. Treatment rooms have positive visualization names like Dignity, Splendor, Wisdom, and Sincerity. The spa's décor mirrors the Japanese, Chinese, Italian, and Victorian influences found in the neighborhoods of San Francisco. Some of the treatment rooms have fireplaces, some have whirlpool tubs, and all incorporate one-of-a-kind cultural accents, such as antique Chinese lanterns and Japanese teapots.

The extensive menu of spa services draws from both Asian and European wellness traditions. Practitioners offer ten different styles of massage, including traditional Swedish, Deep Tissue, and Aromatherapy, as well as more exotic Ayurvedic Dosha Balancing and Balinese Massage. For the Balinese treatment, you lie on a table covered in rose petals and listen to soothing Gamelan music while a massage therapist performs a choreographed rubdown of acupressure, rolling motion, long strokes, and percussive tapping that invigorates the muscles and stimulates blood flow. The Radiant Skin Body Treatments are equally varied—you can choose to have your body pampered with a blend of rice powder and ginger, lavender-infused sugar, or green tea mixed with pulverized apricot kernels.

The latter scrub is particularly lovely, as it finishes with a gentle massage with whipped lime-blossom moisture crème.

For pure luxury, you can't beat the Champagne Facial. Champagne yeast extract has been found to stimulate the skin's metabolism and fight free radicals. In this facial, the extract is combined with antioxidant Chinese herbs to leave your skin radiant and rejuvenated. The spa also offers an innovative Photomodulation Facial that utilizes light-emitting diode (LED) light therapy technology that was first developed by NASA. The theory behind this treatment is that each wavelength of the spectrum provides unique healing benefits. For example, yellow light is said to improve muscle tone and combat the signs of aging and violet light purifies and promotes antibacterial effects, while blue light calms irritated skin and reduces swelling. For lasting improvement, it's best to book a series of these high-tech treatments, but you'll likely see results after even one.

You can lounge all day at the spa, ordering breakfast or lunch from the Big Four Restaurant's special spa-cuisine menu and having your meals delivered to enjoy poolside, in the fireplace lounge, or outside on the terrace. Cozy in a plush white terrycloth robe, you'll feel deeply renewed as you sip a passionfruit-wild berry-ginseng smoothie or nibble on succulent Vietnamese prawn and summer vegetable spring rolls. The distinct pleasures of the historic Huntington Hotel and the contemporary Nob Hill Spa combine to perfectly capture the cosmopolitan spirit of San Francisco.

THE DISTINCT PLEASURES OF THE HISTORIC
HUNTINGTON HOTEL AND THE CONTEMPORARY
NOB HILL SPA COMBINE TO PERFECTLY CAPTURE
THE COSMOPOLITAN SPIRIT OF SAN FRANCISCO.

casa madrona hotel & spa

Casa Madrona was built in 1885 as the home of wealthy lumber baron William Barrett. The epitome of luxury in its day, this sky-blue Victorian mansion is perched high on a Sausalito hillside overlooking Richardson's Bay, Belvedere Island, and the San Francisco skyline. Since 1910, when the house was transformed into a hotel, the property has been a favorite weekend getaway destination for San Francisco couples. Picturesque Sausalito is perhaps one of the most romantic towns in America, and this inn takes full advantage of its setting. Over the years, sixteen New England–style cottages were scattered

about the property and in 2002, a contemporary wing of guestrooms was built, along with the intimate Avanyu Spa.

The sixty-three guestrooms have something of a split personality. Those in the historic mansion and the cottages are decorated in the manner of a whimsical bed and breakfast, while the new rooms are uniformly chic and modern. The original Victorian rooms have ornate antiques, stained-glass windows, and clawfoot bathtubs. Each cottage has a unique theme, ranging from British country manor to artist's loft (with easel and paints) to Himalayan retreat (complete with hookah pipe). The contemporary rooms have sleek mahogany four-poster beds and spacious marble bathrooms. Many of the rooms on the property feature private decks, whirlpool baths, gas or wood-burning fireplaces, and dramatic views of Sausalito harbor. Meandering brick-laid paths adorned with flowers and fountains connect the various rooms and cottages.

The name of the hotel's lively restaurant, Poggio, comes from the Italian for "a special hillside place." Popular with both tourists and locals, the restaurant serves authentic Tuscan fare—fresh pastas, wood-fired pizzas, meats, and seafood roasted on a rotisserie grill—and fine Italian wines. A little California cuisine sneaks into the menu with the seasonal salads, such as the winning winter composition of endive and arugula sprinkled with soft bits of creamy gorgonzola, balsamic marinated figs, and toasted walnuts. The sidewalk café tables out front are prime spots for people watching.

At the heart of Casa Madrona's 2002 expansion was the Avanyu Spa, whose eight treatment rooms are clustered around a charming interior courtyard dotted with terra-cotta pots filled with geraniums, lavender, and rosemary. *Avanyu* is a Tewa Native American name for a mythical water serpent who represents the restorative life-giving power of water. Inspiration for many of the spa's treatments comes from the magnificent beauty of the San Francisco Bay Area, especially from the calming and centering qualities

of the trees found in the Marin County region. The spa embodies this theme with pinecones, seashells, wild grasses, and paintings by local Sausalito artists adorning the treatment rooms and lounge.

The spa's two signature treatments are the Madrona Evergreen Honey Wrap and the Woods and Sea Salt Scrub. The Madrona Evergreen Honey Wrap starts with an invigorating full-body dry brush scrub, followed by a warm, custard-like honey body mask. While you are cuddled in blankets as the moisturizing mask seeps into your skin, a massage practitioner tends to any tension in your neck and scalp. The treatment finishes with the light mist of a Vichy shower and a massage with jasmine-scented oil. The equally pleasant Woods and Sea Salt Scrub uses a synergistic blend of evergreen and sea salt to exfoliate your skin, ending with an herbal moisturizing cream. Both treatments leave your skin soft and smooth.

The spa's massage therapists are trained in a variety of techniques, including long, fluid Swedish effleurage, deep tissue strokes, gentle prenatal massage, soothing aromatherapy, and revitalizing reflexology. Estheticians offer six kinds of facials, customized to your skin type. If your skin is sun damaged, they might suggest the Antioxidant Facial, or if it's oily, the Clarifying Seaweed Facial, a bubbling seaweed mud that exfoliates while it detoxifies and balances your complexion. Men benefit from the Gentleman's Facial, which uses lemon-lime and rosemary-scented products to help counteract the effects of shaving and reduce the signs of aging.

While you won't find any recreational or fitness facilities here, there's plenty of sightseeing and strolling to be done right outside the doors of Casa Madrona. Sausalito is full of art galleries, little shops, cafés, and quirky houseboats. The romantic and creative setting makes for a lighthearted spa escape.

THE ROMANTIC AND
CREATIVE SETTING MAKES
FOR A LIGHTHEARTED
SPA ESCAPE.

the carneros inn

Founded in 2003, the Carneros Inn is situated amidst 27 acres of rolling vineyards in the heart of Napa Valley's bucolic Carneros wine-growing district. Morning fog, cool bay breezes, minimal rainfall, and shallow clay soil define this unique viticultural area that produces some of the nation's finest sparkling wines, Chardonnay, and Pinot Noir. The Inn's design both reflects and respects the agricultural heritage and unspoiled beauty of the land, and its owners help sustain the environment by employing sophisticated water recycling technology and geothermal heating and cooling systems throughout the property.

The resort's style has been dubbed "agricultural chic" for its quirky mix of rustic farm iconography and luxe contemporary décor, as well as for its organic spa treatments. Barnlike structures painted charcoal gray, burnt orange, and pale mint house the lobby, spa, and restaurants. Eighty-six individual cottages comprise the guest accommodations, which look like bunkhouses with their corrugated metal roofs and fences and down-home front porches outfitted with folksy rocking chairs. The sleek, light-filled interiors tell a different story, however. *Au courant* cowhide-covered Corbusier chaise lounges, classic leather club chairs, and cushy beds teeming with pillows make for refined and elegant quarters. French doors open to ultra-spacious private gardens, each with a gas-fired patio heater to make the outdoor living space comfortable for dining and lounging even on chilly fall nights.

Cottage bedrooms feature polished cherry wood floors, flat-screen plasma televisions, and wood-burning fireplaces. Reproductions of vintage snapshots culled from the photo albums of local old-timers adorn the walls. The bathrooms are lavish retreats unto themselves, with mossy-green heated-slate floors, blood orange–scented toiletries, and showers that sport four showerheads (overhead, hand-held, and side spraying), plus a rain shower on the back deck that cascades warm water down onto your body outdoors in the sunshine or under the stars. While it is best to unplug from your cares on a spa vacation, if staying in touch with home is important, the leather-top desk, front porch, and back patio are all fitted with Ethernet ports connected to the inn's high-speed data network.

Tens of thousands of plant species can be found throughout the grounds at the Carneros Inn, including an abundance of fruit and nut trees, herbs and flowers. You can pick pomegranates or figs on your way to the pool or while away the afternoon reading a novel in the apple orchard, which grows seven kinds of apples. The inn's two restaurants make the most of the fresh seasonal bounty. Perched atop the resort's highest elevation, the Hilltop Dining Room, accessible only to guests, takes in panoramic views of the neighboring vineyards. The French-inspired cuisine highlights Napa flavors with dishes such as Pinot Noir–braised lamb shank, goat cheese polenta, and Chardonnay-poached halibut fillet with spring peas, baby carrots, fava beans, and wilted greens.

A short stroll down the hill from the inn, the Boon Fly Café, located on the highway at the entrance to the property, is open to both guests and the general public. Named for a Carneros pioneer who planted orchards and vineyards in the mid-1800s, the café serves rustic country fare, such as lamb hash with poached farm eggs and a side of homemade donuts for breakfast, and beer-battered fish and chips with malt vinegar and fresh tartar sauce for lunch. You can also ask the café staff to pack you a picnic lunch to take with you on a hike or a visit to area wineries. Both of the resort's restaurants feature a wide selection of Carneros wines, as well as special small-lot wines from throughout the world.

The spa at the Carneros Inn offers treatments inspired by and derived from the abundant natural resources of the region. The spa services are categorized by distinctive wine country themes: "The Farms" offers the natural hydrating benefits of dairy products

in such treatments as Soothing Goat Butter Wrap and Warm Goat's Milk Manicure and Pedicure. From lemongrass to olives, "The Harvests" treatments use herbs, fruits, and flowers for healing. "The Wine Cellars" treatments incorporate grapes, such as the Grape Seed and Guava Body Scrub, which uses native grape seeds to exfoliate, red vine leaf extract to improve circulation, and a mixture of oxidant-fighting minerals to restore energy to your skin. "The Minerals" treatments include the Carneros Healing Gem and Stone Massage, which uses solar-charged aromatherapy oils and smooth warm and cold volcanic stones to massage your body while seven semiprecious gems rest on your chakra points to bring mind, body, and spirit into balance. Lastly, "The Creeks of Carneros" bathing treatments are conducted in two outdoor tubs on the spa's deck. These custom-built tubs are lined with heated river rocks and jets that propel the water over your shoulders and out an infinity edge, giving you the sensation of bathing in a creek.

Enjoyed in the privacy of your own guest cottage, the most luxurious spa treatment is the Red Flower Body Ritual. Designed to energize and stimulate blood flow, this seven-part, two-hour ritual is based on the Japanese approach to relaxation and purification. First you unwind in the alfresco shower by washing with mimosa sea algae. Afterward, the masseuse welcomes you into the serenity of the cottage for a gentle rubdown with a gingergrass bamboo scrub to stimulate blood flow as well as energize and firm your skin, followed by a wild cherry blossom rice buff to nourish and soften it. This is followed by a reviving and replenishing rose camellia plum soft water mist, an antioxidant that reduces the effects of the harsh waters on your body. A massage with wild lime oil warms your skin and creates a lasting glow. You then bathe in a mint mineral bath soak that is said to draw the water's energy into your skin. The treatment concludes with a soothing plum blossom silk cream generously applied to your body.

At the Carneros Inn, the objective is to surrender to the wine country's gentle rhythms and pleasures—fine local wines, artisanal cheeses, just-picked apples, and vineyard-themed spa treatments. From the time you arrive to the moment you rest your head on the pillow for the night, you are surrounded by reminders to slow down and appreciate the gifts of the earth.

macarthur place inn & spa

SONOMA, CALIFORNIA   UNITED STATES

MacArthur Place is a historic country inn located in the picturesque northern California town of Sonoma. It is within driving distance of thirty wineries and four blocks from Sonoma Plaza, where you'll find fashionable boutiques, art galleries, and restaurants. Sonoma Valley wineries may not be as famous as those in neighboring Napa Valley, but they are equally enjoyable to visit—and you can do so without the traffic jams and tasting-room crushes that cause so many headaches on the other side of the Mayacamas Mountains.

David Burris, a prominent farmer with nine children, built the original MacArthur Place manor house in the mid-1800s. At that time, the estate was part of a 300-acre working ranch and vineyard, home to cattle, fruit orchards, a hay crop, and many prized trotters used for transportation during the horse-and-buggy era. Wooden pegs and square nails were used in the construction of the stately white mansion, which is set off from the street by a classic picket fence. Five generations of the Burris family occupied the property before its conversion into a luxury inn in 1998. Today, the twenty buildings that comprise MacArthur Place maintain the architectural integrity of the original structures, with Greek Revival Victorian-style architecture, including individually hand-carved spindles on the porch and balcony railings, and forest-green shutters to match those of the original mansion.

Though the architecture of MacArthur Place is Victorian, the interior décor in the sixty-four guestrooms and suites is sophisticated French Country—fancy, but not fussy—with rustic pine furnishings, sumptuous custom-designed duvets, and original paintings by local artists, plus a decadent collection of red wine grapeseed toiletries. All of the guestrooms have high ceilings and large windows, and are individually painted the shades of the wine country color wheel—mustard yellow, dusty rose, cocoa bean, and olive green. In addition, the suites have wood-burning fireplaces, forty-jet hydrotherapy tubs, six-speaker surround sound systems, and patios or balconies overlooking the lush grounds.

Six acres of gardens wend through the property. The original owners of MacArthur Place were avid gardeners, and magnolia and crepe myrtle trees and wisteria vines in the garden date back more than a century. Flagstone walkways lead you past hedgerows, fountains, and myriad sculptures to a small swimming pool and whirlpool. Sequestered seating nooks create a sense of tranquility, privacy, and timelessness, and delightful surprises lurk around virtually every turn, such as six-foot-tall steel daffodils, a swing made from an old ski-lift chair, and a sycamore tree decorated with eight birdhouses. The orchard has twelve different kinds of fruit trees, and in season the harvest finds its way into the pies made in the inn's restaurant, Saddles.

   True to its name, Saddles is located in the historic barn on the estate, and is decorated with all things equestrian, from saddles to cowboy boots to ropes and bridles. Known for its outstanding selection of Sonoma and Napa Valley wines and for its huge and potent martinis (which are shaken, never stirred), the authentic steakhouse serves up corn-fed prime beef, classic appetizers, and oversized side dishes. For starters, you might dig into the jumbo shrimp cocktail, red cornmeal haystack onion rings, or a wedge of iceberg lettuce topped with blue cheese dressing. Entrées include steaks and filets, barbecued ribs, a Black Angus burger, and half a roasted chicken. On the side, go for the sinful potatoes au gratin or give a nod to your diet with a heaping plate of steamed broccoli. Traditional spa food this is not! You may as well just give in and round out the meal with a decadent dessert like the Bailey's brownie mousse parfait.

MACARTHUR PLACE IS
ABOUT AWAKENING
YOUR SENSES AND
IMMERSING YOURSELF
IN THE VERY ESSENCE
OF SONOMA.

While MacArthur Place's restaurant doesn't have much truck with fresh produce, the horticulturally themed Garden Spa is a virtual ode to nature, with whimsical touches such as sinks made out of terra-cotta flowerpots and sunflower-shaped showers. Treatments take place in seven indoor treatment rooms and two outdoor Japanese teahouses, and are grouped into categories such as fruit, flowers, herbs, and earth, rather than the traditional categories of massage, facials, and body care. Many of the treatments use ingredients from the spa's botanical garden, including sage, chamomile, rosemary, geranium, lavender, peppermint, and rose petals.

The Garden Spa specializes in single-note aromatherapy treatments rather than blended fragrances, so you can experience the unique qualities of each essential oil. The refreshing Sweet Orange Massage, for instance, is said to relieve anxiety and inspire joy, while the Chamomile Massage comforts and calms the nervous system. Several signature treatments, including Lavender Dreams, the Rose Garden, and Red Red Wine, involve baths, scrubs or wraps, and massages, all scented with a single fragrance.

The Grape Stomp treatment is offered during the wine country's summer harvest season. This novel treatment begins with an exfoliating foot scrub composed of red wine, grapeseed, mud, and salt. Next, you place your feet in a wine barrel and stomp red wine grapes in order to blend the juice and skins with the scrub for further exfoliation. The treatment ends in one of the outdoor Japanese teahouses, where you relax with a complete foot reflexology massage. MacArthur Place is about awakening your senses and immersing yourself in the very essence of Sonoma.

salish Lodge & spa

SNOQUALMIE, WASHINGTON   UNITED STATES

Set at the top of 270-foot Snoqualmie Falls, Salish Lodge & Spa is a popular weekend getaway spot for Seattle residents. The Snoqualmie Tribe (a subgroup of the Coast Salish Tribe) and other Native Americans of western Washington are said to have considered these thunderous falls a place of great spiritual power. Derived from a Salish word meaning "moon," the name *Snoqualmie* refers to the valley's early residents, who reportedly threw stones into the water as an offering to the Moon Goddess. Today, polished black river stones called "Salish love rocks" adorn the lodge's dining room tables, guestrooms, and spa as romantic tokens of the region's mystical past.

In 1916, the Snoqualmie Falls Lodge opened on the site of the present Salish Lodge & Spa, which became famous in the early 1990s as the location for David Lynch's cult TV series *Twin Peaks*. Renamed the Great Northern Lodge, the hotel's exterior was featured extensively in the series. The nearby town of North Bend pays homage to the program with "Twin Peaks Days" held every August. You can visit Twede's Café, where Agent Cooper regularly enjoyed "cherry pie and a damn fine cup o' joe."

Just a 35-minute drive from Seattle, this Pacific Northwest destination at the foothills of the Cascades feels as if it's a world away. Surrounded by hiking trails—from novice nature trails to seriously squirrelly scrambles—each season the resort's staff selects the area's best trails to show you the Northwest at its finest, highlighting alpine lakes, rivers, and waterfalls. Hikes accent lush fern groves in spring, strolls by cool rivers in summer, stunning colors in the fall, and snow-capped peaks in winter. The lodge offers both guided and self-guided hiking and mountain biking expeditions, as well as all-inclusive fly fishing, rock climbing, whitewater rafting, and kayaking adventures.

The lodge's woodsy palette of warm browns and simple Arts & Crafts–style furnishings complement the natural scenery. The ninety-one guestrooms and suites are designed for romance, with wood-burning stone fireplaces, oversized whirlpool baths, feather beds, and balconies or window seats. You have your choice of nine kinds of pillows, from buckwheat and lavender–filled ones to nonallergenic Swedish foam and pillows with assorted percentages of goose feather and down. In addition to a standard mini bar, you'll find a "spa bath bar" that includes eucalyptus and sage massage oil, candles, incense, and other sensuous treats.

The Salish Spa, which is tucked up on the fourth floor of the lodge, is a silent facility. To maintain an atmosphere of meditative serenity, the spa management asks that you speak softly, just above an intimate whisper, during your stay. The resulting Zen temple mood is enhanced by beautiful Japanese shoji screens, floors inlaid with slate and madrona, and an aromatic cedar ceiling that feels like a protective forest canopy. An extra hour is built into each appointment, so that you have time to sip green tea in front of a crackling fire in the spa sitting room or partake in the warm soaking pools that face floor-to-ceiling vistas of the forest treetops.

In addition to various facials, massages, and body treatments, the spa offers several packages designed for couples. The Rekindle Ritual takes place in a fireside couples treatment suite, with side-by-side massage tables. A 100-minute-long sensory journey, it begins with a relaxing footbath, continues with a lemongrass body scrub, then a shared shower, and ends with a stress-melting heated river rock massage. The Essence of the

FULLY SATED AND RELAXED, YOU'LL RETURN TO
YOUR ROOM AT NIGHT AND BE LULLED TO SLEEP
BY THE DISTANT ROAR OF SNOQUALMIE FALLS.

Earth Ritual follows a similar progression, substituting an "earth cocoon" mud wrap for the lemongrass exfoliation.

Spa staff members take special pride in their Heated River Rock Massages. Each massage practitioner uses a set of rocks that they personally selected based on their distinct shapes and perceived cosmic energies. The potency of the stones is maintained by regularly "recharging" them with fresh air and sunlight.

A rewarding and unique spa experience, the Salish Couples Guided Massage is a private massage class that introduces you to the wonder of nonsexual massage as you explore the intimacy of your partner's sensual touch as a practitioner. Each session is customized to your life—whether you would like to learn a massage technique to alleviate tension from working at a computer all day, or discover how to help heal an injury.

Meals at the Salish Lodge are leisurely affairs. Each day begins with the legendary four-course country breakfast that's been the talk of the town for generations. It includes a berry parfait, old-fashioned steel-cut oats, buttermilk pancakes, and eggs with smoked bacon, pork-apple sausage, honey-cured ham, and more.

Each of the property's three restaurants overlooks the water. The outdoor Kayak Café is open during summer for gourmet burgers and regional microbrews. Upstairs, the Attic Bistro serves fresh Mediterranean fare, providing a cozy place to sip hot buttered rum over the holidays or cool down with a refreshing peach-and-amaretto-flavored Salish Mist after a hot summer hike. Downstairs, the Dining Room is the most formal culinary venue, though Washington State is so casual that dressing up here just means wearing clean fleece. The restaurant's Pacific Northwest–French cuisine, however, is plenty sophisticated. You can savor artisanal cheeses and dishes like Eastern Oregon "Côte de Boeuf" with foraged mushrooms, or Douglas fir–roasted wild salmon with a pine-syrup glaze. The Dining Room's wine list is fifty pages long and specializes in California, Oregon, and Washington wines. Dessert options include warm Fuji apple consommé with coconut sorbet and spun sugar and a crisp pear filled with Bavarian chocolate mousse and slivers of candied orange.

Fully sated and relaxed, you'll return to your room at night and be lulled to sleep by the distant roar of Snoqualmie Falls as whitewater tumbles over granite cliffs into the emerald river canyon below.

The chrysalis inn & spa at the pier

BELLINGHAM, WASHINGTON   UNITED STATES

A chrysalis is about transformation: a golden-colored pupa, wrapped in its cocoon, transforms itself into a butterfly. More generally, the word also refers to a sheltered state or stage of being. All of these notions apply to the Chrysalis Inn, where the tranquil waterfront setting and spa induce such peace of mind that you will emerge from a stay here feeling like a butterfly.

The inn is located four blocks from Bellingham's historic Fairhaven village, a bustling waterfront community that went bust after losing the rail terminus to Seattle in 1892. The turn-of-the-century brick buildings

now house cafés, bookstores, and galleries that showcase the creations of local potters and woodworkers. It is an ideal base from which to explore the region's miles of scenic hiking and cycling trails. Bicycles, kayaks, and canoes are available for rent in the village.

Built in 2001, the Chrysalis Inn's sleek contemporary architecture has been described as "Scandizenian" for its Scandinavian-like clean lines and respect for natural materials combined with Asian forms and accents. The spirit of the Pacific Northwest, however, is fully present as well—manifested in the extensive use of native woods, including Douglas fir, hemlock, and black mahogany, and through the glass walls and large windows that suffuse nearly every room with all-encompassing views of Bellingham Bay and the San Juan Islands. Even on rainy days, the inn glows with warmth and natural light.

The staff at the inn's stylish Fino Wine Bar & Restaurant pride themselves on taking as much of the pretense out of wine tasting as possible. This is a bar for wine lovers, not wine snobs. While there are some California and Washington State selections on the wine list, the focus is primarily European, as is the food served in the restaurant. Fino showcases a rotating selection of aperitif, dessert, and table wines, each of which is sold by the taste, the glass, or the bottle. The "taste" size (about one third of a glass) is a pleasant option if you wish to sample a variety of wines without suffering undue consequences. In order to offer every wine by the glass, the bartenders use a high-tech wine preservation system that employs a vacuum to prevent oxidation after a bottle is opened. A bank of refrigerators adjusted to different settings ensures that each wine is served at its optimum temperature.

The bistro's eclectic European menu includes Spanish tapas, Italian antipasti, French charcuterie, and Hungarian paprika beef stew, among other classic continental specialties. In keeping with the inn's homey atmosphere, binoculars, reading glasses or sunglasses, and patio coats are available for diners to borrow free of charge. The "library" section of the restaurant (complete with shelves of wine-related books and magazines and a roaring fire) is a comfy place to savor dessert, whether a fruit and cheese plate, homemade ice cream, or the daily chocolate special. Bellingham is in the heart of berry country, and many Fino desserts incorporate fresh-picked raspberries, strawberries, and blueberries. The inn also brews good, strong coffee, a vital requirement of the local populace, as the Bellingham region happens to hold the record for the most drive-up espresso stands per capita in Washington. More than fifty stands dot the landscape, with names such as "Brewed Awakening," "Shot in the Dark," and "Well Latte Dah."

The Spa at the Pier is a haven for sensory transformation, created with rich blond woods, amber, mauve, and sage–painted walls, dark slate floors, and muted lighting. Many of the therapeutic treatments use products based upon ocean elements. For instance, in the Oceanic Detox Wrap, blue and brown seaweeds, known for their nourishing and detoxifying properties, are mixed into a fine paste and applied to the body head to toe. These seaweeds, along with the soothing heat of a thermal blanket, promote perspiration and stimulate the metabolism. At the end of the treatment, a cooling moisturizer leaves you feeling purified and restored. Other ocean-derived treatments utilize seawater, salt,

SURROUNDED BY THE INN'S COCOON-LIKE COMFORTS, YOU'LL FEEL YOURSELF GROW MORE AND MORE SERENE AS WAVES LAP THE ROCKY SHORE.

minerals, and self-heating sea foam mud. The mud produces a stimulating bubbling effect as soon as it touches your body. Its warmth helps the active ingredients penetrate the tissue, resulting in deep muscle relaxation.

The spa's estheticians offer a dozen different kinds of facials, including ones designed to treat acne, rosacea, dehydration, fine lines, and wrinkles. Massage therapists provide a wide range of services as well, including Swedish, prenatal, and hot stone techniques, as well as a Raining Water Massage that incorporates warm water cascading from an overhead Vichy shower.

Hydrotherapy treatments, such as the Ancient Oceans Bath, Seaweed Bath, and Moor Mud Treatment, are conducted in a 214-jet tub that delivers a gentle yet highly effective massage. To enhance the experience, the spa staff recommends that all baths be followed by at least twenty minutes in the relaxation room, wrapped up in a spa robe and blanket in front of the fireplace. This quiet lounge faces a little meditation garden and is stocked with herbal tea, lemon water, and assorted nuts and dried fruits.

Guestrooms and suites at the Chrysalis Inn are bathed in subtle earth tones and feature fine linens, down duvets, and gas fireplaces. Two-person soaking or whirlpool tubs either overlook the bay or feature a built-in cherry wood shoji screen that opens to the fireplace and picture window. Daybed window seats outfitted with silk pillows and a cozy throw invite you to put your feet up and enjoy the living tapestry of fishing boats, sailboat regattas, cormorants, seagulls, herons, and seals. Surrounded by the inn's cocoon-like comforts, you'll feel yourself grow more and more serene as waves lap the rocky shore.

The Inn at Langley & Spa Essencia

LANGLEY, WASHINGTON   UNITED STATES

The Inn at Langley is located on Whidbey Island, 30 miles north of Seattle on Puget Sound. Whidbey is one of the largest islands in the continental United States, measuring 45 miles in length, but never more than a few miles wide. Poet Alicia Vogl Sáenz describes the landscape as being "just how [you] imagine the Pacific Northwest: firs, maple, cedar and fern, banana slugs, moss, 40 shades of green, and rain, rain, rain." For more than twenty-five years, the Inn at Langley's owners, former Seattle mayor Paul Schell and his wife Pam, have retreated to the island to recharge after a hard work week

FROM YOUR PRIVATE DECK, YOU CAN WATCH
THE SUN RISE ABOVE THE SNOW—CAPPED
CASCADE MOUNTAINS ON THE MAINLAND,
AND SET OVER THE PASSAGE.

in the city. The deep peace that comes from watching the water and the slow pace of island life always sends them back to the city renewed. They established the inn in 1989, adding the spa a decade later in order to share their favorite place with others.

The island features all the classic elements of Pacific Northwest living—oysters on the beach, blue herons on the tide flats, blackberries in summer, chanterelles in fall, deer grazing, eagles circling, otters playing, and salmon returning. The town of Langley, on the southern end of the island, is picture postcard–quaint, with a permanent population of just 959 people. During the day, you can walk along the beach, linger in a café or at the ice cream parlor, or browse in the bookstores, art galleries, and antiques shops. At night, there's little to do in the sleepy hamlet beyond taking in a movie at the historic Clyde Theatre or having a beer at the Doghouse Tavern.

The Inn at Langley, a lovely four-story Craftsman-style building with cedar shingles, is situated on a bluff overlooking Saratoga Passage. The twenty-six guestrooms and cottages each have 180-degree waterfront views and a whirlpool tub for two that faces both a fireplace and the sea. The décor combines rustic native woods with a simple, chic Asian sensibility. From your private deck, you can watch the sun rise above the snow-capped Cascade Mountains on the mainland, and set over the passage. In spring, you can watch for migrating gray whales. The rooms are so close to the water that you can even hear the *whoosh* sound of the whales spouting.

At the heart of the inn is the Chef's Kitchen Restaurant, which overlooks a formal herb garden and features a massive double-sided stone fireplace and open display kitchen. Every morning, guests enjoy a sumptuous breakfast buffet of fresh-baked muffins and pastries, fruit, and quiche. On weekends, the chef prepares an elaborate, not-to-be-missed six-course dinner featuring Whidbey Island's freshest seasonal ingredients accompanied by premium Washington State wines. As decadent and sensuous as a spa treatment, these meals encourage you to slow down and truly savor both the flavors and the moment.

Homespun and low-tech, Essencia Spa, situated on the beach level of the inn, focuses on bodywork-based therapies. You come here for a good massage, not for high-style beauty treatments. The three massage rooms are modestly adorned with pumpkin-colored walls, pine furnishings, and tabletop fountains. Specialties include Swedish, Hot and Cold Stone, Bodywork for the Childbearing Year, deep tissue, Lomi Lomi, and craniosacral treatments. For the Swedish and deep tissue massages, you can choose from three blends of aromatic oils: relaxing lavender, muscle-relieving birch, or warming cedar-orange. Bodywork for the Childbearing Year utilizes a variety of techniques to meet the needs of pregnancy and to help restore a new mother to physical and emotional balance after her baby is born. This treatment incorporates a special blend of essential oils known to be safe for pregnant women, including lavender, geranium, rosewood, bergamot, lemon, and mandarin orange.

Wet treatments take place in a private steam bath "rain room," and include a Citrus Body Polish, Aromatherapy Wraps, a Seaweed Body Mask, and a Sea Clay Gel Body Mask. Massage practitioners also offer what they call the Essencia Massage Facial. Since they are not licensed estheticians, the treatment is more a relaxing facial massage than a results-oriented facial. If you desire extractions or peels, however, they can refer you to an esthetician in town. When you book a series of treatments at the spa, the management arranges for a single practitioner to take care of you the whole time. This policy allows for a very personal, unhurried experience that is utterly in keeping with the gentle rhythms of life on Whidbey Island.

The Fairmont Empress & Willow Stream Spa

VICTORIA, BRITISH COLUMBIA   CANADA

Named for the Empress of India, Queen Victoria, this eight-story, ivy-clad château opened its doors on January 20, 1908, serving as a destination point for ocean travelers aboard Canadian Pacific steamships. Overlooking Victoria's spectacular Inner Harbor, the hotel is located next to the Royal British Columbia Museum and Parliament Buildings, and just steps away from downtown boutiques and cafés. The genteel city of Victoria, situated at the southern tip of Vancouver Island, is renowned for its British charm, formal gardens, and balmy year-round climate.

Throughout its history, the Fairmont Empress has played host to kings, queens, presidents, and many other illustrious guests. For example, in 1919, Edward, Prince of Wales, waltzed into the dawn in the Crystal Ballroom—an event considered by Victorians to be of such importance that almost fifty years later, the obituaries of elderly women would appear under such headlines as "Mrs. Thornley-Hall Dies. Prince of Wales Singled Her Out." As with many castle-like properties, there are rumors that the hotel is haunted; it is said that the ghost of an early twentieth-century chambermaid shows up now and again on the sixth floor to help with the cleaning.

The hotel's interior remains a grand showplace of regal tapestries, crystal chandeliers, marble fireplaces, and hardwood floors made of exotic woods imported from around the globe. The 472 rooms and suites are decorated with antique furnishings and rich fabrics that recall a bygone era of luxury. There are ninety different room configurations, some more choice than others. The Fairmont Signature and Gold Harbor View rooms are the fanciest, with lofty ceilings and windows overlooking the water.

The Fairmont Empress provides guests with four dining options, depending on your mood. Kipling's, with its bright yellow walls and collection of whimsical teapots, is the spot for casual family dining and is famous for its extravagant Sunday brunch buffet. The Colonial India–themed Bengal Lounge features a Bengal tiger skin (allegedly a gift from the King of Siam) mounted above the fireplace, and 12-foot windows show off majestic views of the harbor and the hotel's rose garden. The restaurant is popular for its authentic curry buffet and long list of signature martinis and cocktails. On weekends, a jazz combo plays, and a special dessert buffet called "Death by Chocolate" tempts adventurous diners.

For a more intimate experience, you can dine by candlelight and firelight in the Empress Room as a harpist strums romantic tunes nearby. This atmospheric restaurant feels like a sophisticated Edwardian gentlemen's club with its tapestry-covered walls and ornately carved ceiling that appears to be mahogany, but is in fact made of plaster and horse hair. The restaurant features innovative seasonal menus of British Columbian cuisine and a five hundred–bottle wine list. Entrées include Pacific rockfish marinated in Kafir lime and ginger served with black bean–glazed bok choy and sweet coconut and banana sticky rice, or ravioli stuffed with smoked ricotta, caramelized root vegetables, and preserved lemon served with a five-herb, white bean, and mascarpone fondant and roasted red pepper syrup.

No visit to the Empress is complete without experiencing Afternoon Tea in the Tea Lobby. More than one hundred thousand people enjoy this noble Victorian tradition each year. Tea includes fresh fruit with Chantilly cream; miniature crustless sandwiches of smoked salmon and cream cheese, carrot and ginger, and egg salad and cucumber; and fresh scones, homemade preserves, and thick clotted cream. A selection of pastries and teacakes rounds out the meal. Empress Tea (a secret blend of teas from Kenya, South India, Assam, Sri Lanka, and China), served on Royal Doulton china, accompanies all courses.

In 2002, the elegant Willow Stream Spa was installed on a quiet subterranean floor of the hotel. The $7 million facility features several fountains, a Romanesque mineral bath, tons of gleaming marble, and a computerized lighting system synchronized to the Victoria sky that changes four times daily to simulate natural light. According to the resort, the name "Willow Stream" embodies the strength of the willow, which carries nourishment

THE SPA'S TREATMENTS
CAPTURE BOTH THE GRACE
OF VICTORIA AND THE SPIRIT
OF VANCOUVER ISLAND'S
NATURAL SPLENDOR.

from the earth, and the flowing journey through life leading to insight and rejuvenation that a stream symbolizes.

The spa's treatments capture both the grace of Victoria and the spirit of Vancouver Island's natural splendor. For example, the signature Island Senses Experience takes you on a two-hour metaphorical journey through the island's coast, forest, and mountains, beginning with an invigorating "salts of the sea" body scrub, followed by an aromatic pine hydrotherapy bath and a detoxifying mud wrap, and ending with a lavender massage, scented with flowers harvested from the fields of Victoria. Other treatments employ locally grown chamomile, rosehip oil, and buckets and buckets of fresh rose petals.

Victoria boasts at least a dozen golf courses, so the spa tends to fans of the sport with a Golf Facial, which uses maple-derived products to moisturize, repair, and protect golfers' skin from the sun and other outdoor elements. The facial is combined with a shoulder, hand, and foot massage to loosen muscles and release tension, so it not only protects and revitalizes the face, but takes care of tired hands and feet as well.

Other intriguing facials include the Willow Stream Marine Energy Facial, which incorporates protein-rich caviar, and the "Fit for a Queen" Facial Experience, which pays homage to the hotel's regal past by using a line of skin care products reportedly favored by members of the Royal Family. "Fit for a Queen" includes treatment with warm towels infused with therapeutic essential oils, such as ylang ylang, tea tree, and lavender, and a gentle massage to increase their absorption, finishing with a hydrating cream mask. At the enchanting Empress, no matter what spa experience you choose, you can count on receiving the royal treatment.

Tigh-Na-Mara
seaside spa resort

PARKSVILLE, BRITISH COLUMBIA   CANADA

Since the 1940s, generations of families have flocked to Tigh-Na-Mara for summer and holiday vacations. The rustic resort is located near Parksville on Vancouver Island's sheltered east coast, an area renowned for its mild year-round climate, abundant wildlife, and wide, sandy beaches on the placid shores of the Strait of George. A Scottish owner named the original cabin *Tigh-Na-Mara* (Gaelic for "House by the Sea") because the setting reminded her of her native homeland. The 22-acre property, flanked on one side by Rathtrevor Beach and on the other by a forest of fir, arbutus, and cedar trees, now boasts 192 handcrafted log buildings.

Lodging options range from stand-alone cabins in the woods to lodge rooms to oceanfront condominiums. In keeping with the resort's camplike atmosphere, the décor is country casual and comfortable. All accommodations have at least one fireplace (either gas or wood burning), and most have a kitchen as well as an outdoor barbeque grill and picnic table. Should you wish to dig for clams or harvest oysters for your supper, the front desk staff can supply you with fishing licenses, buckets, and rakes, as well as cornmeal to clean the bivalves and a few tasty recipes to cook up your haul.

The 16,000-square-foot Grotto Spa at Tigh-Na-Mara, opened in 2003, is one of the largest spas in Canada. Appearing from the outside like a big log cabin, inside is a sophisticated and luxurious haven for grown-ups. Its centerpiece is a swimming pool–sized mineral pool fortified with imported minerals and trace elements from the Sarvar Springs of Hungary. These potent waters are said to be beneficial for tired or sore muscles, back pain, arthritis, eczema, and other ailments. Amazingly realistic-looking faux granite boulders, waterfalls, and ferns surround the pool, while an underwater stereo system pipes in soothing classical music to listen to while you soak and swim.

The spa's treatment rooms are painted shades of dark green and brown to echo the colors of the surrounding forest. All treatments incorporate high-end European spa products with natural minerals, muds, algaes, essential oils, and salts. The menu of services includes an array of massage techniques, facials, scrubs, wraps, and herbal and mineral bath treatments called "kurs," as well as four different kinds of pedicures. The Seaside Pedicure incorporates seaweed, seawater, and spirulina; the Eucalyptus Foot Therapy Pedicure begins with a salt scrub, followed by a eucalyptus foot soak and an energizing reflexology massage; the Sports Pedicure, meant for runners, soccer players, or people who stand on their feet all day, soothes and revitalizes tired callused feet. Lastly, the Mint Garden Pedicure features a peppermint foot scrub, a warm Moor mud foot wrap, and a peppermint oil massage, ending with an application of peppermint foot cream. This pedicure feels like walking through a mint garden on a warm summer day.

APPEARING FROM THE OUTSIDE LIKE A BIG LOG CABIN, INSIDE IS A SOPHISTICATED AND LUXURIOUS HAVEN FOR GROWN–UPS.

The Grotto Spa Signature Experience Facial is both sublimely pampering and dermatologically sound. The 100-minute treatment incorporates a eucalyptus-scented footbath and salt scrub, myrrh toenail treatment, scalp massage, Chinese acupressure facial massage, and contour lifting technique, as well as a thorough course of cleansing, exfoliation, and conditioning for your face.

You can spend all day at the spa, enjoying a light lunch in the lounge. The spa's dining menu includes the Grotto Club (smoked chicken, crisp bacon, lettuce, and tomato with red pepper mayo on herb focaccia bread); low-carb wraps filled with roasted mushrooms, chicken breast, or shrimp; and mixed green and spinach salads. Or you can dine at either of the resort's two restaurants, the Cedar Dining Room or the Copper Lounge. The Cedar Dining Room serves classic Pacific Northwest cuisine, with specialties including house-smoked salmon, warm scallop salad with pancetta bacon, or pork medallions in a sauce made from maple syrup, onion, mushroom, Dijon mustard, cream, and sherry with a side dish of herb spatzle. Coffee toffee torte and an apple and cranberry crisp made with buttery oats and almonds and topped with vanilla bean ice cream are among the dessert offerings. The Copper Lounge serves appetizers, sushi, cocktails, and British Columbian wines.

During the summer, Tigh-Na-Mara organizes daily children's activities such as swimming lessons, sandcastle-building competitions, nature walks, and karaoke parties. Horseshoe pits, a basketball hoop, ping-pong tables, beach volleyball courts, and a host of other amenities entertain both children and adults year-round. Nature, however, provides the most fascinating show. The resort is a bird watcher's paradise. Over 250 species of birds call this region home, including trumpeter swan, loon, brambling, and crested myna. And when the tide rolls out, you and yours can explore tidal pools teeming with sand dollars, tiny fish, crabs, and starfish.

kingfisher oceanside resort & spa

COURTENAY, BRITISH COLUMBIA   CANADA

Kingfisher Oceanside Resort lies just south of Courtenay in Comox Valley on the eastern coast of Vancouver Island. This picturesque region is known for its small towns, farms, and forested parks. Nearly every room in the resort takes in awe-inspiring views of the tranquil waters of Gartley Bay, the northern Gulf Islands, and the snow-capped Coastal Mountains on the mainland. The property is home to an abundance of marine wildlife, including its namesake kingfisher birds, as well as blue herons, cormorants, trumpeter swans, and brant geese. In the spring, dozens of baby bald eagles flock daily to the resort's beach to eat in the rock pools at low tide.

A laidback seaside ambience permeates every corner of this establishment; its sand-colored buildings blend unobtrusively with the coastal landscape, and groovy sculptures and benches made of driftwood dot the grounds. You can elect to stay in either a lodge-style oceanview guestroom or in a beachfront suite. The guestrooms are equipped with pine furnishings, microwaves, mini refrigerators, and private balconies or patios. The suites feature sea-toned furnishings, two televisions, beach rock fireplaces, full kitchens, heated tile floors, and spacious decks perched above the beach. Many of the suites have romantic two-person whirlpool tubs graced with fluffy white towels folded origami-style into swan shapes.

To create its ever-changing, eclectic menu, the casual Kingfisher dining room draws on fresh seafood caught by local fishermen and organic vegetables from local farms as well as from the chef's personal herb and vegetable garden. For starters, you might try panfried Fanny Bay oysters harvested a few miles down the road, or Komoukway button mushrooms stuffed with shrimp, crabmeat, and fine cheeses, baked golden brown on a cedar plank. Hearty entrées include slow-roasted lamb sirloin and black bean and winter squash risotto; lighter options include wild salmon firecracker rolls glazed with sweet chili and lime or curried chicken wraps served in tomato tortillas, filled with tender chicken breast, shredded carrot, sunflower sprouts, and pineapple tossed with curried coconut milk dressing and toasted almonds.

The resort's West Coast Spa, founded in 1999, was the first full-service oceanside spa in Canada. The 8,000-square-foot, three-level facility specializes in spa therapies that draw upon the rich ingredients of the sea. Underscoring this theme, stenciled patterns of

A LAIDBACK SEASIDE AMBIENCE PERMEATES EVERY CORNER OF THIS ESTABLISHMENT.

starfish, scallops, moon snails, and clamshells decorate the spa walls. Treatments include an indigenous Vancouver Island clay wrap, a facial that relies on mineral-rich marine proteins to deliver anti-aging benefits to the skin, a rejuvenating seaweed wrap, and a hot stone massage that uses stones collected from the shore. A tableau of clamshells and smooth gray stones placed underneath the massage table's face cradle is a peaceful reminder of the majestic nature that surrounds you.

In 2003, the West Coast Spa expanded its offerings to include the innovative Pacific Mist Hydropath. Spa director Lori Nawrot was inspired by the thalassotherapy spas of France that harness the unique healing power of seawater. She thought the European spas were too clinical, however, so she set out to create a hydrotherapy circuit that would reflect the environment of British Columbia. The result is a series of rooms that look like sandstone caves and grottos. An indoor path leads you on an hour-long journey through monsoon-like showers, relaxing saltwater and sea mineral pools, stimulating massage pools and waterfalls, detoxifying seaweed and mud tidal pools, a steam cave, and a simulated river walk that produces a "Kneipp" effect for your legs, helping them feel lighter and rejuvenated. The Hydropath offers the many benefits of hydrotherapy—remineralization, detoxification, and relaxation—with the added calming beauty of a seaside tidal setting. This novel spa experience is designed to be shared between family members or friends.

Another recent addition to the property is the Starfish Yoga Studio. Nestled near the beach in front of the spa building, this room is naturally elegant with sand tones, a soft cork floor, an inlaid starfish made with cherry wood, and a fireplace for cool fall and winter mornings. As a yoga teacher instructs you to stretch, you gaze out enormous picture windows to the water and remember to breathe.

the wickaninnish inn & ancient cedars spa

TOFINO, BRITISH COLUMBIA   CANADA

The Wickaninnish Inn is located on Vancouver Island's magnificently wild and rugged west coast near the quaint township of Tofino. Situated on a rocky promontory on Chesterman Beach, The Wick (as it is affectionately called by locals) is surrounded by the Pacific Ocean on three sides, with a backdrop of old-growth temperate rainforest. Low-key and casual, Tofino is populated mostly by fishermen, loggers, hippies, and surfers. The region is so remote that in the summertime, you see black bears contentedly munching fistfuls of dandelions by the side of the road.

The Wick's managing director and co-owner, Charles McDiarmid, grew up in Tofino; his father was the town's sole doctor. As an adult, McDiarmid left Vancouver Island and forged a distinguished career working for Four Seasons Resorts, but he always dreamed of returning home to establish a rustic, yet refined small hotel. In 1996, he finally achieved his dream, building the inn on land that had been in his family since the early 1970s. The name Wickaninnish, taken from a nearby bay, literally means "He who no one sits in front of in the canoe" in the native Tha-o-qui-aht language, but it was actually the name of the most powerful chief in the area at the time of the first contact with the Europeans.

The hotel is composed of two three-story weathered cedar buildings that complement the natural beauty of the setting. The first thing you notice upon entering any of the seventy-five guestrooms and suites is the spectacular ocean view revealed by floor-to-ceiling picture windows. You can step out onto a private balcony, breathe in the fresh salt air, watch bald eagles and ospreys circle overhead, and listen to the waves crash onto the rocks below.

Everything about the interior décor reinforces the sense of place. The furnishings are fashioned from recycled old-growth fir, western red cedar, and driftwood. The wool sisal carpet looks like ripples in the sand at low tide and the bathrooms are tiled with ocean-green slate and tile. Barnacle-encrusted stone votive candle holders rest on the rough-hewn cedar mantelpiece. The rooms are thoughtfully appointed with binoculars, raingear,

field guides to the local flora and fauna, and aromatherapy bath salts to enjoy in the deep soaker tub. There's even a CD player with a collection of albums by Canadian artists, such as Diana Krall (who grew up on the island), Sarah McLachlan, and Shania Twain.

While there are no children's activities per se here, the resort is very family friendly. Several suites are outfitted with kitchens and loft beds, and you can arrange for the "Kids Night In" package that includes a babysitter, room service, and a children's movie on DVD. The guest services representatives at the concierge desk are exceptionally friendly and helpful. They can plan a three- or four-day custom itinerary for your stay, tell you about the galleries and restaurants in town, book a whale-watching expedition for you, or ensure that a candlelit drawn bath is awaiting you upon your return from dinner, accompanied, if you wish, by a bottle of chilled champagne.

During the winter, the inn offers special Storm Watching packages, as the west coast of Vancouver Island receives some of the most intense squalls in all of North America. From the cozy comfort of your soaker tub, you can watch the spectacle of 20-foot waves pounding onto the coast.

The inn's Pointe Restaurant and On-the-Rocks Bar and Lounge are cantilevered above the surf. The hand-chiseled cedar post-and-beam construction features soaring 20-foot ceilings and a circular wood-burning fireplace with a copper hood and chimney. Outdoor microphones connected to speakers in the restaurant pipe in a symphony of

croaking tree frogs and the sound of the waves as you dine. The menu showcases fresh seafood, including Fanny Bay clams, gooseneck barnacles, and wild salmon, along with other Vancouver Island specialties, such as venison carpaccio, lemon-glazed duck breast, and an excellent selection of Pacific Northwest wines. For dessert, you might consider the passionfruit custard flan or the Belgian chocolate mousse "lasagna" served with port wine and vanilla-infused oranges. During the warm summer season, the restaurant also hosts a fun crab cookout on the beach three times a week.

The Ancient Cedars Spa is nestled on the ground level of the inn, within spray distance of the waves. All spa treatments begin with a soothing footbath either seated by the fireplace in the lounge or outside on the patio surrounded by ferns and evergreens. First your massage practitioner or esthetician gives you all sorts of heavenly aromatherapy oils to smell and helps you decide which one best suits your mood, and then pours a few drops of the scent into a copper basin filled with hot water, sea salts, and marbles (which act as a little self massage for your feet). You soak and meditate for about 20 minutes, feeling yourself decompress and transition into an open, spa-ready state.

You can choose from a variety of massages, body wraps and polishes, facials, nail treatments, and hydrotherapy baths. The Cedar Sanctuary treatment cottage is an especially romantic place to receive a side-by-side massage with a loved one. This rustic structure made of cedar, spruce, fir, and yew wood smells like the forest and opens to the sea.

THE WICKANINNISH INN IS AN IDEAL PLACE TO REFLECT UPON THE PAST AND CHART NEW BEGINNINGS.

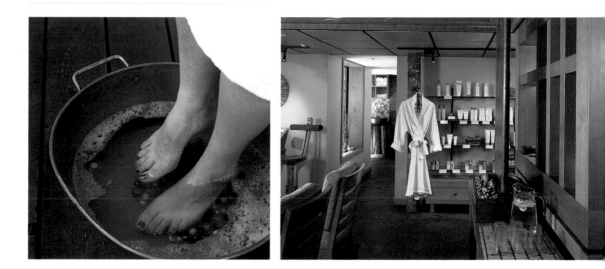

The spa's signature experiences include a Hot Stone Massage and Hot Stone Facial. The facial uses heated basalt stones and cool marble stones in a Swedish-style massage to stimulate circulation, detoxify the skin, and improve muscle tone. The stones used in both of these treatments are harvested from the beach in Tofino and energized, according to the spa manager, with the cycles of the moon.

The massage practitioners specialize in temple-style Lomi Lomi massage, which is traditionally used by Hawaiian shamans during rite-of-passage ceremonies. You can elect to undergo this ritual with either one or two practitioners—if possible, definitely opt for the transcendental four-hands version. The experience begins with a Kahi Loa prayer that involves light touch, guided imagery, and chanting related to the elements of Fire, Water, Stone, Plant, Animal, and Wind. Then the ritual moves on to a weaving of passive movement, stretching, and rhythmic whole-body massage strokes that release tension on many levels. The deeper meaning of Lomi Lomi is to remove that which does not belong, and thus to awaken the senses to harmony. With its intimate proximity to nature and tranquil interior design, the Wickaninnish Inn is an ideal place to reflect upon the past and chart new beginnings.

clayoquot wilderness resorts & spa

TOFINO, BRITISH COLUMBIA   CANADA

The Clayoquot Wilderness Resorts experience unfolds at two locations: The Floating Resort at Quait Bay and the Wilderness Outpost at Bedwell River. Both destinations are situated on sheltered inland waters near Tofino on the west coast of Vancouver Island. The Clayoquot Sound, which has been designated an official biosphere reserve by UNESCO, is like a prehistoric Garden of Eden, with glistening primordial forests, mist-shrouded fiords, and crystalline glacial waterfalls. Breathtakingly beautiful and achingly pure, the landscape is one of the few remaining stretches of temperate rain forest on earth.

Black bears, cougars, deer, elk, eagles, seals, otters, puffins, sea lions, whales, and myriad other wild creatures make the Sound their home. The only way to get here is by boat, floatplane, or helicopter.

Snuggled up against the Quait Bay shore, the Floating Resort is constructed on a former coal barge. The intimate lodge has just sixteen guestrooms, a library lounge, fireside bar, fitness room, and barrel-vaulted dining room. The interior has a north woods cabin look, with rough cedar walls, cedar furniture, and distinctive First Nations (indigenous tribes) art. The guestrooms are simply but sumptuously appointed with plush towels, down comforters, and private decks adorned with hanging baskets of flowers. By design, there are no televisions or phones in the guestrooms to distract you from the magnificent bay and mountain views. The water is so clear that you can peer through its glassy surface and see starfish, sea anemones, and all manner of jellyfish. If need be, however, there is a satellite television in the lounge and access to the Internet and a cell phone in the office.

The Floating Resort is connected to the shore by a little bridge. The Healing Grounds Spa, built in 2002, resides amidst lush fern gardens and ancient cedars, and features an alfresco lakewater shower, a waterfall-fed pool, steamy cedar hot tubs, and secluded outdoor massage platforms. A one-of-a-kind rainforest sauna with soothing overhead mist delivers a contemporary interpretation of the ceremonial sweat lodge, a cleansing ritual practiced by the native Nuu-Chah-Nulth peoples in the area.

Indoors, the spa reflects its natural surroundings through the use of warm woods and polished slate. Artful collages of twigs, leaves, and shells decorate the walls. The spa services menu focuses on relaxing massages, including aromatherapy, Swedish,

deep tissue, hot stone, shiatsu, and pre- and postnatal techniques. The two-hour Complete Body treatment, which involves a foot soak, a head-to-toe dry brush exfoliation, and the massage style of your choice, is a popular indulgence. Many of the treatments, such as the Seaweed Foot Retreat, incorporate local seawater and seaweed. Salt glows, glacial clay wraps, paraffin dips for hands and feet, and botanical facials round out the spa offerings.

At the conclusion of your treatment, your practitioner will invite you to rest on the meditation deck overlooking the water and forest. She will wrap you in a goose down duvet and lead you outside to cocoon in a lounge chair, where you will be served a relaxing cup of tea such as Mountain Berry, a blend of Saskatoon berries, currants, raisins, Seneka root, and blueberries, or Lemon Verbena Blend, which is said to inspire lemon-drop sweet daydreams.

On clear days, morning yoga classes are held outside on the deck. On rainy days, they are moved to the cedar longhouse, where heated slate floors and a 12-foot-wide copper-hooded indoor fire pit create a beguiling sanctuary.

The other Clayoquot property, the Wilderness Outpost, is located about 20 minutes by boat from the Floating Resort at the mouth of the Bedwell River Valley. While the enclave is modeled on the late eighteenth-century tradition of Great Camps, this is grand twenty-first-century safari-style camping, as the resort meets strict contemporary standards of luxury despite its remote location. The enchanting tone is set when Pete and Poke, a sibling team of Norwegian draft horses, meet you at the dock and carry you and your bags in their handcrafted parade wagon up to the compound.

The accommodations consist of sixteen white canvas tents set on cedar platforms with private verandahs. Furnishings include beds fashioned out of alder branches, wing-backed velvet chairs, and Persian rugs. Lace tablecloths, oil lamps, and bouquets of wildflowers top antique dressing tables. On chilly nights, remote-controlled propane stoves

keep you toasty. Each tent has its own composting toilet and mirrored sink in a separate cedar outbuilding. Windmills and solar energy power the lights and hot water heaters. In addition to the guestroom tents, there are two dining tents, two massage tents, a games tent, and library lounge tent, each outfitted in authentic vintage splendor.

Whether you are young or old, an expert outdoors person or not, the possibilities for adventure are endless in this wilderness paradise. An enthusiastic team of knowledgeable activity leaders and affable guide dogs stand at the ready at both locations to ensure your safety and pleasure. Popular activities are horseback riding, hiking, and mountain biking, but sailing, kayaking, canoeing, fishing, gold-panning, whale watching, and more are available.

Dining at Clayoquot Wilderness Resorts has nothing to do with any childhood memories you may have of campground cookouts. Forget about hotdogs and beans. The first dinner course here, for example, might be a house-smoked wild Pacific salmon and chive ravioli, followed by an oven-roasted breast of muscovy duck served with sweet potato shallot custard and honey-braised Belgian endive with pan jus. Next might come an after-dinner salad of organic dandelion greens and wild mushroom ragout. Dessert, if you have room, could be a cinnamon-spiced salmonberry cobbler with warm maple crème anglaise or homemade vanilla bean ice cream with blueberry compote. All courses are paired, if you wish, with the finest British Columbian wines and a charming running commentary by the sommelier.

After dinner, you might retire to the library for a snifter of sherry and a good book or to the games tent for a round of chess or old-fashioned snooker. Millions of stars in the inky black Clayoquot sky will bid you a brilliant good night.

PRACTICALITIES & SPLENDID DETAILS

BERNARDUS LODGE

415 Carmel Valley Road
Carmel Valley, California 93924
United States

U.S. TOLL-FREE: (888) 648-9463
TEL: (831) 658-3400
FAX: (831) 659-3529
WWW.BERNARDUS.COM

ACCOMMODATIONS:
57 Rooms

CUISINE: 2 Restaurants

SPA & FITNESS FACILITIES:
8 Treatment Rooms; Hair and
Nail Salon; Sauna; Steam
Room; Gym; Swimming Pool;
Hot Pool

SIGNATURE TREATMENTS:
Après Golf Massage; Vineyard
Romance Experience

CLASSES: Culinary and
Viticulture Seminars;
Meditation, Personal Training;
Stretch; Yoga

ACTIVITIES & NEARBY
ATTRACTIONS: Bocce Ball;
Golf; Hiking; Horseback
Riding; Lawn Croquet; Tennis;
Monterey Bay Aquarium;
Antiques Shops and Wineries
in Carmel Valley

SPECIAL NOTES: Rose Garden
hosts weddings nearly every
weekend

GETTING THERE: 20-minute
drive from Monterey
Peninsula Airport; 2-hour
drive from San Francisco

CAL-A-VIE

29402 Spa Havens Way
Vista, California 92084
United States

U.S. TOLL-FREE: (866) 772-4283
TEL: (760) 945-2055
FAX: (760) 630-0074
WWW.CAL-A-VIE.COM

ACCOMMODATIONS:
24 Cottages

CUISINE: 1 Restaurant

SPA & FITNESS FACILITIES:
10 Treatment Rooms; Hair
and Nail Salon; Hot Tub;
Sauna; Steam Room; Gym;
2 Swimming Pools

SIGNATURE TREATMENTS:
Aromatherapy Massage;
Magnetic Therapy

CLASSES: Aerobic Dance;
Body Sculpting; Cardio
Kickboxing; Circuit
Training; Mat Pilates; NIA
(Neuromuscular Integrative
Action); Nutrition; Spinning;
Stress Management; Tai Chi;
Water Volleyball; Yoga;
and more

ACTIVITIES & NEARBY
ATTRACTIONS: Golf;
Hiking; San Diego; Walking
the Labyrinth

SPECIAL NOTES: 3-, 4-, and 7-
night all-inclusive packages;
guests must be over age 15;
special theme weeks
throughout the year geared
toward foodies, mothers and
daughters, men, breast cancer
survivors, brides-to-be, and
more

GETTING THERE: 45-minute
drive from San Diego
International Airport

THE CARNEROS INN

4048 Sonoma Highway
Napa, California 94559
United States

TEL: (707) 299-4900
FAX: (707) 299-4950
WWW.THECARNEROSINN.COM

ACCOMMODATIONS:
77 Rooms; 9 Suites

CUISINE: 2 Restaurants

SPA & FITNESS FACILITIES:
6 Treatment Rooms; Hot Tub;
Nail Salon; Sauna; Steam
Room; In-Room Services;
Gym; Swimming Pool

SIGNATURE TREATMENTS:
Red Flower Body Massage
Ritual; Soothing Goat Butter
Wrap

CLASSES: Yoga on Weekends;
periodic writing retreats

ACTIVITIES & NEARBY
ATTRACTIONS: Bicycling;
Bird Watching; Canoeing;
Hiking; Wineries in Napa
Valley and Sonoma Valley

SPECIAL NOTES: The resort
regularly hosts private wine-
tasting parties for guests with
local winemakers

GETTING THERE: 1-hour
drive from San Francisco

CASA MADRONA
HOTEL & SPA

801 Bridgeway
Sausalito, California 94965
United States

U.S. TOLL-FREE: (800) 567-9524
TEL: (415) 332-0502
FAX: (415) 332-2537
WWW.CASAMADRONA.
ROCKRESORTS.COM

ACCOMMODATIONS:
56 Rooms; 7 Suites

CUISINE: 1 Restaurant

SPA & FITNESS FACILITIES:
8 Treatment Rooms; Steam
Room; In-Room Services

SIGNATURE TREATMENTS:
Madrona Evergreen Honey
Wrap; Woods and Sea Salt
Scrub

CLASSES: None

ACTIVITIES & NEARBY
ATTRACTIONS: Hiking;
Kayaking; Bay Area Discovery
Museum; Fisherman's Wharf
in San Francisco; Galleries,
Houseboat Tours, and Shops
in Sausalito; Muir Woods;
Yacht Charters

SPECIAL NOTES:
Babysitters available

GETTING THERE: 45-minute
drive or ferry ride from San
Francisco

THE CENTURY PLAZA
HOTEL & SPA

10220 Constellation Boulevard
Century City
Los Angeles, California 90067
United States

TEL: (310) 277-2000
FAX: (310) 551-3355
WWW.SPAMYSTIQUE.COM

ACCOMMODATIONS:
683 Rooms; 41 Suites

CUISINE: 2 Restaurants

SPA & FITNESS FACILITIES:
27 Treatment Rooms;
4 Outdoor Treatment Cabanas;
Hair and Nail Salon; Hot Tub;
Sauna; Steam Room; Gym;
Swimming Pool

SIGNATURE TREATMENTS:
Korean-Style Akasuri Scrub;
Thai Massage

CLASSES: Body Sculpting;
Cardio Salsa; Cardio
Sculpting; Core Conditioning;
Mat Pilates; Stability Ball;
Stretch; Tai Chi; Water
Aerobics; Yoga

ACTIVITIES & NEARBY
ATTRACTIONS: Beaches;
Shops on Rodeo Drive and
at Century City Shopping
Center; Getty Museum;
Touring Broadway
Productions at the Shubert
Theatre; Universal Studios

SPECIAL NOTES:
Pets allowed

GETTING THERE: 25-minute drive from Los Angeles International Airport

THE CHRYSALIS INN & SPA AT THE PIER

804 10th Street
Bellingham, Washington 98225
United States

U.S. TOLL-FREE: (888) 808-0005
TEL: (360) 756-1005
FAX: (360) 647-0342
WWW.THECHRYSALISINN.COM

ACCOMMODATIONS:
34 Rooms; 9 Suites

CUISINE: 1 Restaurant

SPA & FITNESS FACILITIES:
7 Treatment Rooms;
Nail Salon; Steam Room

SIGNATURE TREATMENTS:
Ancient Oceans Therapeutic
Bath; Anti-Aging Aqua Facial

CLASSES: None

ACTIVITIES & NEARBY
ATTRACTIONS: Board
Games; Bicycling; Golf;
Hiking; Kayaking; Shops and
Restaurants in Fairhaven
District

SPECIAL NOTES: You can
order a glass of wine to sip
while you get your nails done

GETTING THERE: 1½-hour
drive from Seattle; 1-hour
drive from Vancouver

CLAYOQUOT WILDERNESS RESORTS & SPA

P.O. Box 130
Tofino, British Columbia
Canada V0R 2Z0

U.S. TOLL-FREE: (888) 333-5405
TEL: (250) 726-8235
FAX: (250) 726-8558
WWW.WILDRETREAT.COM

ACCOMMODATIONS:
16 Rooms; 16 Tents

CUISINE: 2 Restaurants

SPA & FITNESS FACILITIES:
3 Treatment Rooms; 2 Massage
Tents; Hot Tub; Outdoor
Massage Platforms; Nail Salon;
Sauna; Steam Room; Gym

SIGNATURE TREATMENTS:
Complete Body Treatment;
Seaweed Foot Retreat

CLASSES: Yoga

ACTIVITIES & NEARBY
ATTRACTIONS: Bicycling,
Canoeing; Fishing; Hiking;
Horseback Riding; Kayaking;
Ocean and Fresh Water
Fishing; Whale and Bear
Watching

SPECIAL NOTES: Quait Bay is
open April through November;
Wilderness Outpost is open
May through September;
3-, 4-, and 7-night all-inclusive
packages available. If you have
time, opt for the combination
deal that includes both
locations

GETTING THERE: 50-minute
flight from Vancouver to
Tofino or 35-minute flight or
5-hour drive from Victoria to
Tofino, followed by 30-minute
boat ride from Tofino to
Clayoquot Wilderness Resorts

THE FAIRMONT EMPRESS & WILLOW STREAM SPA

721 Government Street
Victoria, British Columbia
Canada V8W 1W5

U.S. TOLL-FREE: (800) 441-1414
TEL: (250) 384-8111
FAX: (250) 381-5959
WWW.FAIRMONT.COM/EMPRESS

ACCOMMODATIONS:
425 Rooms; 47 Suites

CUISINE: 4 Restaurants

SPA & FITNESS FACILITIES:
11 Treatment Rooms; Hair and
Nail Salon; Hot Tub; Sauna;
Steam Room; In-Room Services;
Gym; Swimming Pool

SIGNATURE TREATMENTS:
"Fit for a Queen" Facial
Experience; The Island Senses
Experience

CLASSES: None

ACTIVITIES & NEARBY
ATTRACTIONS: Bicycling
(bike rentals available at
the hotel); Golf; Kayaking;
Afternoon Tea; Shops and
Restaurants in Victoria;
The Butchart Gardens

SPECIAL NOTES: Babysitters
available; small pets allowed

GETTING THERE: ½-hour
flight or 1½-hour ferry ride
from Vancouver; 1-hour flight or
3-hour ferry ride from Seattle

FOUR SEASONS HOTEL LOS ANGELES AT BEVERLY HILLS

300 South Doheny Drive
Los Angeles, California 90048
United States

U.S. TOLL-FREE: (800) 819-5053
TEL: (310) 273-2222
FAX: (310) 859-3824
WWW.FOURSEASONS.COM/
LOSANGELES

ACCOMMODATIONS:
187 Rooms; 98 Suites

CUISINE: 3 Restaurants

SPA & FITNESS FACILITIES:
8 Treatment Rooms; Poolside
Treatment Cabanas; Hot Tub;
Nail Salon; Sauna; Steam
Room; Gym; Swimming Pool

SIGNATURE TREATMENTS:
Deep Skin Ionization Facial;
Punta Mita Tequila Massage

CLASSES: None

ACTIVITIES & NEARBY
ATTRACTIONS: The beach;
Hollywood and downtown
Los Angeles; nearby tennis
and golf clubs

SPECIAL NOTES: Babysitters
available; courtesy stretch
limousine transportation to
Rodeo Drive and to addresses
within a 2-mile radius of the
hotel; kosher kitchen; small
pets allowed

GETTING THERE: 30- to 45-
minute drive from Los Angeles
International Airport

THE HUNTINGTON HOTEL & NOB HILL SPA

1075 California Street
San Francisco, California 94108
United States

U.S. TOLL-FREE: (800) 227-4683
TEL: (415) 474-5400
FAX: (415) 474-6227
WWW.HUNTINGTONHOTEL.COM

ACCOMMODATIONS:
100 Rooms; 35 Suites

CUISINE: 1 Restaurant

SPA & FITNESS FACILITIES:
10 Treatment Rooms; Hot Tub;
In-Room Massages; Nail
Salon; Sauna; Steam Room;
Gym; Swimming Pool

SIGNATURE TREATMENTS:
Green Tea Scrub;
Photomodulation Facial

CLASSES: Ener-chi (fusion of
Chi Kung, Yoga, and Pilates);
Fit Ball; Inner Balance (blend
of Feldenkrais, Alexander
technique, and Meditation);
Pilates; San Francisco Walk;
Yoga

ACTIVITIES & NEARBY
ATTRACTIONS: Chinatown;
Fisherman's Wharf;
San Francisco Museum of
Modern Art; Union Square

SPECIAL NOTES: Babysitters
available; courtesy town car
transportation to Union Square
and the Financial District

GETTING THERE: 30-minute
drive from San Francisco
International Airport

THE INN AT LANGLEY & SPA ESSENCIA

P.O. Box 835, 400 First Street
Langley, Washington 98260
United States

TEL./FAX: (360) 221-3033
WWW.INNATLANGLEY.COM

ACCOMMODATIONS:
22 Rooms; 4 Suites

CUISINE: 1 Restaurant

SPA & FITNESS FACILITIES:
4 Treatment Rooms; Steam
Room; Gym

SIGNATURE TREATMENTS:
Bodywork for the Childbearing
Year; Swedish Massage

CLASSES: None

ACTIVITIES & NEARBY
ATTRACTIONS: Bicycling;
Golf; Kayaking; Scuba Diving;
Shops and Restaurants in
Langley; Whale Watching

SPECIAL NOTES: Be sure to
book your weekend dinner
reservation in advance; no
children under age 12

GETTING THERE: 1^{1}/2-hour
drive (includes ferry ride)
from Seattle

KINGFISHER OCEANSIDE
RESORT & SPA

4330 Island Highway South
Courtenay, British Columbia
Canada V9N 9R9

U.S. TOLL-FREE: (800) 663-7929
TEL: (250) 338-1323
FAX: (250) 338-0058
WWW.KINGFISHERSPA.COM

ACCOMMODATIONS:
28 Rooms; 26 Suites

CUISINE: 1 Restaurant

SPA & FITNESS FACILITIES:
22 Treatment Rooms; Massage
Hut on Beach; Hot Tub; Nail
Salon; Sauna; Steam Bath;
Gym; Swimming Pool

SIGNATURE TREATMENTS:
Pacific Mist Hydropath;
Sea Stone Massage

CLASSES: Couples Massage
Class; Personal Training;
Stretching; Tai Chi; Yoga

ACTIVITIES & NEARBY
ATTRACTIONS: Bicycling;
Fishing; Golf; Hiking;
Horseback Riding; Scuba
Diving; Skiing at Mount
Washington Alpine Resort

SPECIAL NOTES: Pacific Mist
Hydropath requires swimsuit

GETTING THERE: 20-minute
flight from Vancouver to
Comox, followed by 20-minute
drive to Courtenay; 2^{1}/2-hour
drive from Victoria

LAS VENTANAS
AL PARAÍSO

Carretera Transpeninsular Km. 19.5
San José del Cabo, Baja California
Sur C.P. 23400
Mexico

U.S. TOLL-FREE: (888) 767-3966
TEL: +52 (624) 144-2800
FAX: +52 (624) 144-2801
WWW.LASVENTANAS.COM

ACCOMMODATIONS:
61 Suites

CUISINE: 3 Restaurants

SPA & FITNESS FACILITIES:
8 Treatment Rooms (including
4 Cabanas with Private
Gardens); Beach Massage
Pavilion; Hair and Nail Salon;
Hot and Cold Water Pools; In-
Suite Services; Sauna; Steam
Room; Gym; Swimming Pool

SIGNATURE TREATMENTS:
Nopal Anti-Cellulite and
Detox Wrap; Sea and Stars
Night Massage for Two

CLASSES: Chronic Pain
Solution; Mexican Cooking;
Personal Training; Qi Gong;
Stretching; Tennis; Yoga

ACTIVITIES & NEARBY
ATTRACTIONS: Fishing;
Golf; Horseback Riding;
Kayaking; Sailing; Scuba
Diving; Snorkeling; Surfing;
Tennis; Windsurfing.
All-Terrain Vehicle and
Jeep Tours of the Baja Desert;
Night Life in Cabo San Lucas;
Shops in San José del Cabo;
Whale Watching

SPECIAL NOTES: Babysitters
available, pets allowed

GETTING THERE: 15-minute
drive from Los Cabos
International Airport
(San José del Cabo)

MACARTHUR PLACE
INN & SPA

29 East MacArthur Street
Sonoma, California 95476
United States

U.S. TOLL-FREE: (800) 722-1866
TEL: (707) 938-2929
FAX: (707) 933-9833
WWW.MACARTHURPLACE.COM

ACCOMMODATIONS:
34 Rooms; 30 Suites

CUISINE: 1 Restaurant

SPA & FITNESS FACILITIES:
7 Treatment Rooms; 2 Garden
Teahouses; Hot Tub; Steam
Room; Gym; Swimming Pool

SIGNATURE TREATMENTS:
Grape Stomp; Lavender Dreams

CLASSES: None

ACTIVITIES & NEARBY
ATTRACTIONS: Bicycling;
Hiking; Board Games;
Galleries, Restaurants, and
Shops in Sonoma; Historic
Mission San Francisco de
Solano; Hot Air Ballooning;
Wineries in Sonoma Valley

SPECIAL NOTES: Bicycles
available for rent

GETTING THERE: 45-minute
drive from San Francisco

MONTAGE RESORT & SPA

30801 South Coast Highway
Laguna Beach, California 92651
United States

U.S. TOLL-FREE: (866) 271-6953
TEL: (949) 715-6000
FAX: (949) 715-6100
WWW.MONTAGELAGUNABEACH.COM

ACCOMMODATIONS:
211 Rooms; 51 Suites

CUISINE: 4 Restaurants

SPA & FITNESS FACILITIES:
21 Treatment Rooms; Hair
and Nail Salon; Hot Tub;
Sauna; Steam Room; Gym;
3 Swimming Pools

SIGNATURE TREATMENTS:
Aroma-Balancing Therapy;
Montage Anti-Aging Facial;
Surrender Retreats

CLASSES: Beach Bootcamp;
Beachfront Yoga; Indoor and
Outdoor Stationary Cycling;
Meditation; Pilates; Personal
Training; Piloga (fusion of
yoga and Pilates); Tai Chi/Chi
Gong; Thalassic Beach Walk

ACTIVITIES & NEARBY
ATTRACTIONS: Fishing;
Golf; Jet-Skiing; Kayaking;
Sailing; Scuba Diving;
Snorkeling; Surfing; Tennis;
Catalina Island; Galleries
and Shops in Laguna Beach;
Whale and Dolphin Watching;
Wineries in Temecula Valley

SPECIAL NOTES: Children's
Club; dogs allowed

GETTING THERE: 30-minute
drive from Orange County's
John Wayne International
Airport; 90-minute drive from
both Los Angeles and San Diego

ONE & ONLY PALMILLA

Carretera Transpeninsular Km. 7.5
San José del Cabo, Baja California
Sur, C.P. 23400
Mexico

U.S. TOLL-FREE: (866) 829-2977
TEL: +52 (624) 146-7000
FAX: +52 (624) 146-7001
WWW.ONEANDONLYPALMILLA.COM

ACCOMMODATIONS:
61 Rooms; 111 Suites

CUISINE: 3 Restaurants

SPA & FITNESS FACILITIES:
13 Private Treatment Villas;
Ocean View Massage Cabana;
Hair and Nail Salon; In-Suite
Services; Sauna; Steam Room;
Watsu Pool; Gym; 2 Swimming
Pools; Yoga Garden

SIGNATURE TREATMENTS:
Aztec Aromatic Ritual;
Palmilla Four Hand Massage

CLASSES: Personal Training; Pilates; Spinning; Tai Chi; Transformational Breath Work; Yoga

ACTIVITIES & NEARBY ATTRACTIONS: Deep-Sea Fishing; Golf; Horseback Riding; Kayaking; Sailing; Scuba Diving; Snorkeling; Tennis; All Terrain Vehicle Tours of the Baja Desert; Night Life and Shops in Cabo San Lucas; Whale Watching

SPECIAL NOTES: Around-the-clock butler service; Children's Program and babysitters available; dedicated children's swimming and recreation area; pets allowed; wedding chapel

GETTING THERE: 25-minute drive from Los Cabos International Airport (San José del Cabo)

■
SALISH LODGE & SPA

6501 Railroad Avenue SE
Snoqualmie, Washington 98065
United States

U.S. TOLL-FREE: (800) 826-6124
TEL: (425) 888-2556
FAX: (425) 888-2533
WWW.SALISHLODGE.COM

ACCOMMODATIONS:
87 Rooms; 4 Suites

CUISINE: 3 Restaurants

SPA & FITNESS FACILITIES:
8 Treatment Rooms; 2 Couples Treatment Suites; Hot Tub; Sauna; Steam Room; Gym

SIGNATURE TREATMENTS:
Couples Guided Massage; Heated River Rock Massage

CLASSES: None

ACTIVITIES & NEARBY ATTRACTIONS: Bicycling; Fly Fishing; Golf; Hiking; Kayaking; Rock Climbing; Whitewater Rafting; Wineries in Columbia Valley

SPECIAL NOTES: Ask for a room with a river view (otherwise you may get stuck looking at the neighboring hydroelectric power plant); bathing suits are required in the co-ed sauna

GETTING THERE: 35-minute drive from Seattle

■
TIGH-NA-MARA SEASIDE SPA RESORT

1095 East Island Highway
Parksville, British Columbia
Canada V9P 2E5

U.S. TOLL-FREE: (800) 663-7373
LOCAL: (250) 248-2072
FAX: (250) 248-4140
WWW.TIGH-NA-MARA.COM

ACCOMMODATIONS:
85 Rooms; 107 Suites

CUISINE: 2 Restaurants

SPA & FITNESS FACILITIES:
15 Treatment Rooms; Decks for Outdoor Treatments; In-Room Services; Hair and Nail Salons; Hot Tub; Mineral Pool; Steam Bath; Access to Nearby Gym; Basketball Hoop; Beach Volleyball Courts; Children's Playground; Horseshoe Pits; Ping-Pong Tables; Swimming Pool; Tennis Courts

SIGNATURE TREATMENTS:
Grotto Spa Signature Experience Facial; Mint Garden Pedicure

CLASSES: Meditation; Yoga

ACTIVITIES & NEARBY ATTRACTIONS: Bird Watching; Bicycling (bikes available for rent at the hotel); Clam Digging; Fishing; Golf; Hiking; Horseback Riding; Kayaking; Whale Watching

SPECIAL NOTES: Babysitters available; bathing suits required in Grotto Mineral Pool; pets allowed (except in July and August); seasonal summer, Easter, and Christmas children's programs

GETTING THERE: 20-minute flight from Vancouver to Qualicum Beach; 2-hour ferry ride from Vancouver to Nanaimo (Duke Point), followed by a 45-minute drive from Nanaimo to Parksville; 2½-hour drive from Victoria

■
VENTANA INN & SPA

Highway 1
Big Sur, California 93920
United States

U.S. TOLL-FREE: (800) 628-6500
TEL: (831) 667-2331
FAX: (831) 667-0573
WWW.VENTANAINN.COM

ACCOMMODATIONS:
38 Rooms; 23 Suites

CUISINE: 1 Restaurant

SPA & FITNESS FACILITIES:
6 Treatment Rooms; Hot Tub; In-Room Services; Sauna; Gym; 2 Swimming Pools

SIGNATURE TREATMENTS:
Energy Work; Color Readings

CLASSES: Meditation; Pilates; Tai Chi; Yoga

ACTIVITIES & NEARBY ATTRACTIONS: Hiking; Horseback Riding; Shops, Restaurants, and Wineries in Carmel Valley; Whale Watching

SPECIAL NOTES: No children under age 17

GETTING THERE: 3½-hour drive from San Francisco; 2½-hour drive from San Jose

■
THE WICKANINNISH INN & ANCIENT CEDARS SPA

Osprey Lane at
Chesterman Beach
P.O. Box 250
Tofino, British Columbia
Canada V0R 2Z0

U.S. TOLL-FREE: (800) 333-4604
TEL: (250) 725-3100
FAX: (250) 725-3110
WWW.WICKINN.COM

ACCOMMODATIONS:
63 Rooms; 12 Suites

CUISINE: 1 Restaurant

SPA & FITNESS FACILITIES:
6 Treatment Rooms; In-Room Services; Nail Salon; Steam Room; Gym

SIGNATURE TREATMENTS:
Hot Stone Massage; Lomi Lomi

CLASSES: Movement Meditation; Pilates; Yoga

ACTIVITIES & NEARBY ATTRACTIONS: Bicycling (bikes available for rent at the hotel); Bird Watching; Fishing; Golf; Kayaking; Surfing; Cougar Annie's Garden; Rain Forest Walks; Tide Pool Exploration; Whale Watching

SPECIAL NOTES: Babysitters available

GETTING THERE: 50-minute flight from Vancouver; 35-minute flight or 5-hour drive from Victoria

ACKNOWLEDGMENTS

Heartfelt thanks to all of the spa and hotel owners, managers, publicists, massage therapists, estheticians, nail technicians, fitness instructors, naturalists, chefs, sommeliers, waiters, bartenders, concierges, butlers, front desk clerks, chauffeurs, housekeepers, and bellhops who made my work on this book such an over-the-top pleasure.

I'm grateful as well to the Canadian Tourism Commission for so generously and efficiently arranging my flights to Vancouver Island. On the home front, *besitos* to Dave and Annalena Barrett, Anne Burt, Susan Davis, and to my agent Amy Rennert for their steadfast support.

Last but not least, I offer my eternal gratitude to editor Lisa Campbell for shepherding this project to fruition with such grace and care and to art director Ayako Akazawa, copy editor Carolyn Keating, and production manager Steve Kim, as well as to Nion McEvoy, Jan Hughes, Doug Ogan, and the rest of the gang at Chronicle Books. They are just the greatest. —G.H.

The photographer wishes to thank his assistants Natalie Darville, Gabriel Branbury, Jeff Johnson, and Brian Johnson. Thanks also to Birte Walter (stylist on The Carneros Inn, Las Ventanas al Paraíso, and One&Only Palmilla) and Pam Caudle (stylist on Ventana Inn & Spa). —C.R.